How to Build an Evangelistic Church

JOHN R. BISAGNO

How to Build an Evangelistic Church

BROADMAN PRESS
NASHVILLE, TENNESSEE

Foreword

The New Testament Church is not dead! Sad to say, in some places it is somewhat anemic. This should not be so. The volume which you hold in your hand is living proof that a real New Testament church should neither be weak nor dead, rather it should be virile, vibrant, and victorious people of God.

John Bisagno has proven to all churches everywhere that a real witness for Christ can be built wherever and whenever God's people major on the primary objectives. God's blessings upon the ministry of this great preacher and pastor prove that the message of Christ is powerful wherever applied. For five years, John Bisagno was pastor of a suburban church. The methods described in this book served to build there one of the greatest churches in the Southern Baptist Convention. A little over a year ago, God moved him to the downtown, First Baptist Church of Houston, Texas. There in a thriving, bustling city of economic and intellectual might, God has used the same methods to produce a twentieth-century miracle. Never have we known anything comparable to the growth experienced in the First Baptist Church, Houston, under John Bisagno's ministry. The same methods worked here as in the previous pastorate. This is the assurance that these methods will be effective wherever applied.

Every pastor and church leader should give prayerful thought and consideration to that "which God hath wrought" as it is unfolded in this book.

James E. Coggin,
Pastor, Travis Avenue Baptist Church
Ft. Worth, Texas

Contents

This has to be. It is what Jesus done

Contents

CHAPTER 1
Depend on God

Let it be clearly understood that the work of our Lord is a spiritual ministry, accomplished by spiritual men achieving spiritual ends. "He who hath begun a good work in you," cried Paul, "will perform it until the day of Jesus Christ." In its inception, continuation, and conclusion it is all of him. He did not say, "Without me ye cannot do much," rather, "Without me ye can do nothing!" Nothing is a contraction of two words—"no" and "thing"—and literally means "a thing which does not exist." That is what we are apart from him. As a bulb can give no light apart from its source of electricity, so we are totally devoid of accomplishing power apart from the source of God. Nothing includes everything. Without him you cannot even exist. You cannot breathe, taste, see, drive, talk, let alone preach or win without him. A thing that does not exist—that is what we are without Christ. Nothing —no thing.

These pages are not intended to be a guaranteed blueprint for instant success. What works for one may not work for another. They will have to be tried, adapted to your particular situation, and sifted through your personality. They are philosophies and methods that fit me. There are, however, some important constant factors in a physical sense that will be common to every situation.

The churches that disbelieve the word of God are cold and dead and are not growing. The great Sunday Schools, the great growing soul-winning churches of America are all conservative, Bible-believing, gospel-preaching, warm-hearted, informal evangelistic churches. They have spirited singing, warm services, and a major on outreach. They all minimize activities. They all major on priorities. The church that intends to grow must keep these factors constant! But, one can do all of these things without the power of God and fail. To depend on him is to succeed.

To make no plan is folly. So plan! Be evangelistic and warm hearted. Work hard. Preach the Word. Major on outreach. Dream. Think. Hope. Make no little plans. But, in all your planning and dreaming as you absorb these methods and philosophies, remember that you must go to your knees daily in prayer. Pray in the services. Pray with the staff. Pray alone. Pray at home. Pray as you drive. Pray everwhere. Work as though it all depends on you and pray as though it all depends on God. Plans and structures are an irreplaceable part of God's work. He may bless you if you make no plans and have no structure, but he can bless you more if you do. A critic once said, "Preacher, I don't like your methods." I replied, "What kind of methods do you use?" "I do not use any methods," he said. "Well," I said, "I like my methods better than yours." These are the methods God has given me. They work for me and I hope they will work for you. As you read remember that without plans, thought, and methods, you will not do much. Without God, you will not do anything!

CHAPTER 2
Instil Vision

It was business as usual. Prayer meeting night in a little suburban church. Five hundred seats, 475 empty, and 25 faithful souls. Lustily the organ cranked on and on, but for all their trying, they just could not get much heart into "Day Is Dying in The West." And brother, that is not all that was dying in the West, and the East, and the North, and the South! Many are dead and just don't know it. Why? There are a hundred reasons. The people stay away in great droves. Ninety-nine percent of America will not be in church next Sunday night. And it is only slightly better on Sunday morning. Any why should they go? Most services are dead, dull, despondent, and depressing. At any ball game, concert, movie, or street fight, there is more life than at the average church. One reason is the absence of vision. There is no life because there is no hope. And there is no hope because there is no expectancy. There is no expectancy because there is no vision. There is no vision because the preacher has not instilled vision and the result is death. *For without vision, the people perish.* Vision, like expectancy, always hopes for something better, always expects it, always believes it will happen. "Can do" is its theme. "The Impossible Dream" its theme song. Its motto, "The difficult we'll do right now, the impossible may take a little while."

For five years at the First Southern Baptist Church of Del City, Oklahoma, every Sunday people by the scores came to Christ and joined the church. For several months during the first year at Houston that intangible something that I wanted, and to which I had become accustomed, was not there. I did not know what it was, but I knew what it was not. Sunday after Sunday I would go home from church and say to my wife: "It was a good service, but it is not the same. It's not right, but I can't put my finger on it." That elusive "something" was missing. One Sunday morning fifty-seven people were saved and joined the church. The next Sunday there were thirty-nine. The following Sunday it happened! That intangible something I had missed was there. I did not know what it was I was looking for until I reviewed that service again and again. The thing that made the difference, expectancy—an air of excitement, hope, vision, expectancy—was in the air. It is there every Sunday now. I realistically know and you know that we will probably never win everyone in Houston to Christ, but I don't want anyone telling my people that. They are almost convinced that they can! They are expecting to do it. They are expecting packed audiences, souls saved, lives changed, fire from heaven every Sunday.

Without let up, Sunday after Sunday after Sunday I preach to them that by virtue of the fact we bear the name "First," it is our responsibility to lead the way, to set the pace in evangelism. Two million persons live in greater Houston. It is the crossroads of the nation, heart of the Americas, gateway to outer space. Revival here will effect the world. Slowly it began to dawn on them that our church must be one of God's great bastions of the gospel. It must be a mighty lighthouse in a mighty city. He has placed us here for a purpose. The time is now. We must set the pace. We must launch out. *Houston must be won for Christ—now!* They began to believe it could happen. The raindrops began to fall. Faith became sight. Dream became reality. Then there was expectancy. They prayed, worked, and expected it again and again. Then the windows of heaven opened and the rains came. "Without a vision, the people perish!"

CHAPTER 3
Assume Leadership

The leadership of the pastor is a very delicate matter. There is a fine line between leadership and dictatorship.

In 1969 the great Travis Avenue Baptist Church of Fort Worth, Texas, conducted a survey of the ten largest Sunday Schools in America and found some constant factors in all of them. They were all conservative and evangelistic. They all preached and believed the Bible was true. They all minimized activity and majored on outreach. and, they all had a pastor who was a strong personality in whom the people had entrusted great leadership. I am not suggesting that a church be a dictatorship. It is a democracy. But, a man must have room to breathe. He must be able to go before the people and say under God, "This is the will of the Father for us." The church, of course, must always give final approval. The time-honored traditions of committee and church action must be followed. but, a pastor must be free as the undershepherd, to lead the flock. They are not to lead him, he is to lead them as God leads them both. For the church to vote on where to place all light bulbs and where to sing each song in the service is absurd. In a recent state convention, in the midst of a heated debate, a pious brother stood and made a motion that the assembly pause for prayer. The presiding officer wisely said, "Thank you brother, but we don't have to vote to pray. It is the thing to do. Let's just pray." As pastor, you should take hold. Assume leadership. You do not have to have a church vote on whether or not to have cocktails at the next Sunday School party, or whether to gamble the church funds on the Kentucky Derby. If the question comes up, tell them no. We are not going to do it. That's all there is to it. It is not right. If it is in the Book, if it is right, don't vote on it, just do it. The matter of voting on every little dinky thing that comes up in many churches has reached the realm of the ridiculous. If the deacons want to steal the evangelist's love offering to pay for the revival expenses, tell them to get lost and give the man his money. If you take it up for him, give it to him. If you take it up for something else, give it to something else. The church does not have to vote whether or not to steal a man's offering. People have no respect for a man who does not know where he is going and does not know where he has been with God. They want leadership. They will not respect nor will they follow wishy-washy leadership that does not lead. Be God's man, but be a man's man too!

A young preacher walked cockily into the pulpit, struck out, and with bowed head, walked out in humiliation. A wise old preacher said to him, "Young fellow, if you would have gone in that pulpit like you came out, you would have come out like you went in." Walk humbly before God, but walk confidently.

Strangely, you may find the laboring man harder to lead than the businessman. A man who himself is a leader is quick to acknowledge, respect, and follow leadership in another. The subjugated man who is suppressed by his superiors at work all day may come to church and want to be a general. He can be the harder man to deal with. But, when he is honored, loved, appreciated, and complimented by his pastor, he too can respond as quickly to his leadership. You must walk with God. Know that your words are his words, your dreams, his dreams. If your life before your people is the kind of life that evokes their confidence, if your plans repeatedly bear the mark of God's obvious blessing and approval, the people will give you leadership. You do not have to ask for leadership. *If you have to ask for it, you do not have it.* You do not have to flaunt it in their faces or tell them you are taking it. *When you have to start reminding them you are the pastor, you no longer are!* Leadership is never demanded, it is earned.

At the beginning of every pastorate there is usually a three- or four-month period when the people are quietly watching and not saying much. It is then that your leadership is on trial. Walk quietly, but prayerfully and confidently before the people. Make your decisions, know they are right, carry them through, and God will confirm your leadership with his blessings and the people will respond. Where there is no leadership, there is chaos and confusion. Where there is no leadership, there is no direction. Where there is no direction, there is no accomplishment. Don't be arrogant, but don't hesitate. If it is right, don't vote on it, just do it.

Revival always starts with one man. Where there is a strong business there is a strong man. Where there is a great movement, there is a great man. To assume leadership is to assume a precarious role. Nobody kicks a dead dog. To enjoy the fruits of leadership is to endure the accompanying perils of criticism, misunderstanding, and loneliness. If you can't take that, then resign yourself to the world of mediocrity. "He who travels fastest, travels alone."

Leadership may often be wrong, but never in doubt. You do not always have to be right, but you do always have to be the pastor.

CHAPTER 4

Listen to Your Critics

Fortunate is the man who has learned that he does not always have to be right. Give the other man credit for his opinion. He too, is an individual. He thinks what he thinks for a reason. His opinions are the product of a combination of factors, all of which may be valid and yet different from yours. If you humble yourself sufficiently to earnestly listen, you may find him to be right. "You know, you may be right," can be the sweetest words to the ears of another man and may do more to elevate you in his opinion than anything else you can do. And, he just may be right too! At least part of it may be right, and coupled with the part you have right, could make for the best.

I have my attitudes on ecology, poverty, welfare, housing, Vietnam, politics, and other issues. But, when I moved to Houston, I determined I would not alienate a possible three-quarter segment of society from my message by not even listening to those who disagreed with me. I do not know everything. I do not have all the facts. I do not have to always be Mr. Right, and neither do you.

Students criticize the church. They say it is highbrow, hypocritical, dull, and irrelevant. It is stained glass, lifeless, meaningless, unimpressive, and unimportant. And the truth of the matter is that in thousands of cases, they are right. In the vast majority of churches it is absolutely that way. But, there are some spots where the church is alive, healthy, vibrant, involved, warm, and compassionate. I tell these young people that if the kind of church you have described is the kind of church you attend, then you are going to the wrong church! On the other hand, remember that you cannot preach to everyone. On the right and left we deal with the entire spectrum of human opinion from the atheist to the tongues talker. Every hue of the rainbow is present in the various shades of contemporary theological thought. Listen to them all, but do not just listen, hear, really hear what they are saying. If it is valid, if it is scriptural, if it is true, acknowledge it, profit from it, and make some changes. If not, throw it out with the rest of the garbage. Do not go to bed to spend a restless night just because someone disagreed with you. Listen to them. Profit from them, and forget it. The other man may have something to contribute. He just could be right.

CHAPTER 5
Motivate the People

Information plus motivation equals action. Is there action in your church? Is there growth, purpose, direction, and accomplishment? Are there results? Is there conquest and achievement? If not, and you are preaching the truth, if you live where there are prospects, and if you are a man of prayer, one of two things is true. There is no information or there is no motivation. In other words, people must know what they are to do and then they must want to do it. The problem is that most of us know to do more than we want to do! We are perhaps the best informed age of Christians in history. We have more education, information, conferences, conventions, clinics, and colleges than any people have ever had. We have more study courses and have won more seals than our forefathers. Multitudes of Christians have covered their walls with seals representing completed study course books. We learn, but we do not accomplish. We comprehend, but we do not do. *We are hearers of the word, but not doers.* Most have won a seal but have never won a soul! While we continue to use these new methods, new soul-winning ideas, and new institutes and tracts to inform the people how to be soul-winners, the truth of the matter is that most of them simply do not want to be soul-winners. They have information but not sufficient motivation. If they had to, most Christians could probably tell someone how to accept Christ as their personal savior. But, they just do not do it. As the most enlightened age in history, it is obvious that the reason we do so little is that information—knowing what to do—is not being coupled with motivation—the desire to do what we know. To know what to do is human. To do what we know is divine.

Motivation. What is it? Recently I flew to Florida. On the plane I chatted with Darryl Royal, Texas University football coach. I asked him to select one word which in his opinion was the major contributing factor to his unparalleled success as a coach. The word—*attitude*. Centuries ago it was said the same way, "As a man thinketh in his heart, so is he." A mediocre football team can beat a better team if it thinks it can. You and your people can do what you dream and plan to do. If you approach a situation with failure in mind, you will fail. Expect, plan, hope, dream. Attitude is so important. If you want to do it, and believe that God wants you to, get your people excited about it and you can do anything. Motivation begins with enthusiasm.

The preacher awoke in the middle of the night to find the church house ablaze. And who should be leading the bucket brigade, throwing water on the fire, but the town atheist! "Atheist," said the preacher. "I've never seen you at church before." "Preacher," said the atheist, "I've never seen your church on fire before!" *Let the church get on fire and the world will come to watch it burn!*

Enthusiasm put John Kennedy in the White House. Enthusiasm builds empires. Enthusiasm makes successes of common men. Enthusiasm wins the day. Enthusiasm does the impossible. Enthusiasm is half the battle. *Enthusiasm motivates.* He who would excite must be excited. A leader must excite people. They have to be revved up, plugged in, turned on, or they won't do anything. Lest you think that I speak of a cheap, hollow, claptrap kind of emotionalism, I would remind you that the very word "enthuse" comes from two Greek words *en* and *theos.* It means simply "in God" and "God in you." "God in you" carries the picture of the lesser containing the greater. It is like two wildcats in a gunny sack. They are too big for it. The result: excitement, enthusiasm, and action!

Secondly, motivation is repetition! Wrigley built an empire on a five-cent package of gum. His advertising philosophy was repetition. Over and over and over again keep before the people the urgency of outreach, the imperative of evangelism. At every gathering, every committee meeting, and every assembly, talk about winning souls. Repeat it again and again. Make it the driving, burning, consuming passion of your people.

In 1960 I walked into a drugstore in Ohio to buy some razor blades. The store was having a sale on peach sundaes. Hundreds of flyers hung from the ceiling. They were everywhere—PEACH SUNDAE 19¢, PEACH SUNDAE 19¢, PEACH SUNDAE 19¢. I went to the counter and took out a dollar to buy razor blades. The clerk said, "What will you have?" I said, "Give me a peach sundae!" I didn't want a peach sundae. I wanted razor blades! But they had convinced me that I wanted a peach sundae. Repetition had won the day!

For years the First Baptist Church of Amarillo has lead the entire Southern Baptist Convention in mission giving through the Cooperative Program. I asked the pastor, Dr. Winfred Moore, for his secret. He told me that for thirteen years he had never preached a sermon on Sunday morning, Sunday night, or Wednesday night without mentioning tithing. Repetition. Repetition. Repetition.

Thirdly, motivation is illustration. Every time I preach I try to mention the name of one of our people who has done something good and use it to motivate others to do the same. When a new convert is introduced, and you know that one of your people has won him, call the person to the front to stand by that new convert when he is presented. Illustrate it to the people. Tell them what others are doing. Suggest that they can do the same thing.

Fourthly, motivation is example. Do it yourself. People are not naive. If you go Sunday after Sunday without converts, the people will begin to wonder why you as pastor cannot at least win one once in a while yourself. Lead the way. Set the pace. Show them how. Jesus said, "Do not let your left hand know what your right hand is doing." But, he also said, "Let your light shine before men." How do you reconcile the two? It is simple. He added, "they may glorify your Father which is in heaven." We motivate others when they see us do it. Only you may know in your heart, however, that it is for his glory and not yourself. If you know it and the Lord knows it, that is all that is important. You need not tell the people, they will know it without being told. The only way to lead someone is to get out in front of them. Be a living example. Lead the way. Set the pace. Do it yourself.

Again, motivation is getting the people to do what they know they ought to do. It is probably 75 percent enthusiasm plus a combination of repetition, illustration, and example. Get excited! Say it again. Talk about others who do it, and do it yourself. In a few months the people will begin to follow!

CHAPTER 6
Major on Outreach

The church more than any other institution in the world does not exist solely for the sake of its membership. It exists to be the salt of the earth, the light of the world, and the redeeming factor in a dying society. To stand still is to go backward. Outreach is the name of the game. Every planning meeting, every teachers meeting, every committee meeting must be conducted in an atmosphere saturated with a constant preoccupation with reaching others. How to get out of the church into the world where the people are to witness, to teach, and to win them. That Sunday School teacher who has not enlisted a new member in a year is doing a bad job. The organization that is standing still is loosing ground.

In 1960 in Japan it took all Protestant denominations together an entire year to win one-twentieth of one day's birth rate. That means if what we believe is true, for every person we won to Christ, over 7,000 died and went to hell. In many cities in America 60 and 70 percent of the teenagers have had experience in dope, premarital sex, drinking, and the rest. How can the church sit idly by and be swallowed up in a sea of drowning souls and not think *outreach!* The YMCA, the Masons, the government, none are charged with the responsibility of winning the lost to Christ. They are all about us. They are everywhere and the job belongs to the redeemed alone. Never be satisfied, always want more, always expect it. Plan for it, push and preach for it. Every assembly, service, meeting, Bible School commencement, girls mission coronation—everything is an opportunity for evangelism. A time to motivate and a time to reap. Influence flows downhill. It starts at the top. If the people are to be constantly and preeminently consumed with a passion for others, it must come from the top. The pastor must preach it, promote it, and practice it. When you throw the dragnet of salvation, expect to catch every variety of fish. *And do not throw any back.* The rich, the poor, the reject, the rebel, the long hair, the short hair, the black, and the white will all come in. The drunk, the addict, the liar, and the adulterer, sensing the genuine love for them, will come to your church. Tell your people they are to expect it. Tell them they are to rejoice in it. This is what it is all about. The worse they are, the more they need to be in church. Jesus repeatedly rebuked the Pharisees for condeming him because he ate, walked, and mingled with the sinners. Hear him as he cries again and again, "They that are whole need not a physician. The Son of man has come to seek and save that which is lost!" We cannot, we must not, we dare not, attempt to minister to a select group. Let the proud and pompous leave if they do not like it. The redeeming message of Christ is to all men everywhere in their sins. There are already enough churches in your town where the spiritual snobs, the proud, and the pious can go. Let them play "high church." Let them be a powerless people with powerless services that change nothing and accomplish nothing. Let them be whited sepulchers. Let them play their little Sunday morning games. Ignore them. Let them leave. But, get together the people of God that love the Lord and love lost souls and get busy about winning the world. *The church is not a showcase for saints. It is a hospital for sinners.*

Hark! 'tis the Shepherd's voice I hear,
Out in the desert dark and drear,
Calling the sheep who've gone astray,
Far from the Shepherd's fold away.

Bring them in, Bring them in,
Bring them in from the fields of sin.
Bring them in, bring them in,
Bring the wand'ring ones to Jesus."

CHAPTER 7
Set Goals and Check Up

God believes in numbers, for numbers represent people. He even named an entire book in the Bible in honor of numbers. The Holy Spirit is always very meticulous in recording numbers. As three stands for the Trinity, six for incompletion, and seven for completion, the use of numbers in the Bible is always very significant. Three thousand were saved on the day of Pentecost. Three hundred composed Gideon's army. Eighty-five thousand were slain in Sennacherib's Army. Seven thousand refused to bow and kneel to Baal.

The man who does not count noses does not know where he is or how he is doing. Every successful venture has a goal and keeps records. If you aim at nothing, you will accomplish nothing. Pray for the mind of God as to what he would have you accomplish. Set your goal, keep good records, and check up on yourself. Set records that are inspiring but realistic. Far better to plan for 1,000 and have 1,050, than to plan for 1,500 and have 1,100. Fifty more might be reached with a more unrealistic goal, but the good will probably be more than offset by the discouraging facts in the remainder of the people. Always aim higher. Always plan to do more. He who dreams no dreams will never see his faith made sight. Make good plans. Check up periodically. Review your progress with your staff and people. If you are not achieving God's goals, make changes of approach. Eliminate what has proven unfruitful and accent what is working. It is a wise coach that alters his game plan if he is loosing the game.

In a day of some encouraging signs with scattered revival here and there, the fact still remains that in every quarter we are falling farther and farther behind the fulfilment of the Great Commission. Our Lord has told us to go into all nations and make desciples of all men. The Great Commission has not been revoked!

CHAPTER 8

Streamline the Organization

Without exception the great Sunday Schools of America and the great soul-winning churches have all established priorities and eliminated much of the lesser important activity. Busyness is often the death knell of the modern church. While it is well to be organized and active, it is possible to relegate the primary into the role of the secondary and organize yourself out of business. Wednesday night must be centered in preparation and outreach for Sunday's day of harvest. Through the years we have found that any week which has a special activity, such as an extra one-night service, a banquet, or a fellowship, will be a week in which other regularly scheduled activities will suffer. People only have so many hours in the week. They do have more to do than go to church. I do not plan to go to church six nights a week for the rest of my life, nor do I plan to ask my people to do so. Christian families must have Christian fellowship together. Homelife, recreation, and other outside interests are important too. Parents should attend their son's football game, or their daughter's high school play. It is imperative that the adult take interest in the activity of the children, and all activities are not, and should not be, centered in the church. A well-rounded life is important. The family that is involved in church activities five or six nights a week may well become a family with problems. Simply because a particular church activity has met on a particular night at a particular time for a particular length of time, does not make it hallowed. The hour meeting could be cut to forty minutes and with proper preparation and efficiency, the thirty-minute meeting could be cut to twenty minutes. Consolidate the activities of Wednesday night. Go over every activity with a fine-tooth comb. Streamline and reorganize, plan, add, and eliminate. In the most ideal situation, everything is involved in two nights weekly—Wednesday and Sunday. In a neighborhood church, it is possible to have all auxiliary meetings, including officers and teachers' meetings, and a Wednesday night meal from 5:30 to 7:00, church-wide visitation from 7:00 to 8:00, and prayer meeting from 8:00 to 8:30. To involve the member on the periphery in visitation, make it easy on him. Give him the opportunity to visit when he will already be at church on Wednesday night. Better to have 200 visit 2 prospects on Wednesday night than the faithful 15 to visit 5 on Monday night.

Give organizations a shot in the arm with periodic single meetings, such as a quarterly visitation banquet or a monthly men's prayer breakfast. But, by all means, streamline the organization.

Take one fourth or one third of the time off each activity and try to consolidate it all into a streamlined, swiftly moving Wednesday night program. Do not drag your people to church four or five times a week. They will be better for it, the kingdom of God will prosper, and you will have time to be a better husband and father as well as pastor.

CHAPTER 9
Capitalize on Problems

If life gives you a lemon, make lemonade. If you will but put your mind to it, you will find that there is probably some way to make an advantage out of your difficulties, an asset of your liabilities.

For uncounted years, First Baptist Church, Houston, has bemoaned the problem of parking. Parking in the inner-city had become such a difficulty that we had actually developed a complex over it. Yet, less than 100 feet from the church's front door, we have free access to a large parking garage. To be sure, there is a bit of difficulty in winding up several stories to park your car, and yet, any other auditorium seating nearly 3,000 persons would have a parking lot that would require walking a block or two to your car. We began to advertise, "Houston's greatest church parking." And indeed it is. For where else can you park 700 cars, all in enclosed parking, 100 feet from your front door? It had just never occurred to us that that parking garage was one of our greatest assets. We simply took that lemon and made it into lemonade.

With the exception of a few permanent residents of hotels, no one lives within five miles of our church. What a lemon! What a problem. And yet, with 250,000 people working within a mile and a half, with businessmen, sales-clerks, secretaries, and uncounted thousands of employees, we realized ourselves to be sitting in the midst of a spiritual gold mine. As our director of ministries said one day, "Pastor, I feel like we are drowning in a sea of souls." A marquee with slogans and announcements of coming events changed daily, a face-lifting for the building, special street ministries to the transient, special witness efforts during peak Christmas shopping times, the accessability to all points of the city by freeways, the ease of travel on Sunday morning, these and hundreds of other small things have turned liabilities into assets and problems into opportunity. There is some problem that is peculiar to your church which could be turned into an opportunity of outreach. Think!

CHAPTER 10
Seize the Opportunity

The creative church administrator will always be on the outlook for that opportunity which may never come again. It may not be obvious at first, but it is usually always there. A sign on the marquee with a comment about a current event may bring a picture to the front page of the local newspaper. A visiting dignitary who is an outstanding Christian in your area for another engagement may be readily available for a Sunday morning testimony in your church. Every day uncounted opportunities to enhance and promote the work of the Lord come within our grasps. See every situation as a chance to spread the word. A speaking engagement in a far distant city when a certain company is transferring hundreds of employees to your city from that one could be most advantageous. Serving on a community project committee with unsaved men could be a grand opportunity for witness.

Encourage converts who have not been baptized by the end of the year to do so on the first Sunday in January. It is not only a fine way for them to begin the new year, but it is a good means of making disciples of converts.

Giving an invitation at a Bible School commencement or GA coronation might not be going by the book, but it could be a golden opportunity to win parents who may attend your church no other time. Visit hot prospects the day after they attend the revival service. Visit good Sunday morning prospects that very afternoon. Keep your eyes open, be alert, strike while the fire is hot, seize the opportunity. Our Lord, who commanded us to be as wise as serpents and as harmless as doves, constantly gives opportunity for us to enhance the work of the Kingdom! With your heart attuned to his Sprit, your eyes and ears open to circumstances, watch and faint not. You may be entertaining angels of opportunity unaware.

CHAPTER 11
Instil Pride

Admittedly the world has a false idea of success when it comes to spiritual matters. Great buildings and great crowds of people do not necessarily mean great success in God's eyes. And yet, we live in a world of men who do have their opinions of success. And people like to be identified with success.

The psychology of the winning football team that brings the crowd in great numbers is undisputed. When my team wins, I win. When my church wins, I win. Nobody likes a loser. Your people will not witness and attend, will not bring their friends, talk up the church and be active if a negative attitude of despair, pessimism, and defeat permeates your church. Clean up the buildings. Paint that old sign. Mow the grass. Shine your shoes. Sharpen up the service. Make your people proud to be Christians, proud of the church, and proud of their pastor. They will identify, they will want to come, and they will want to bring their friends. A man that is whipped and discouraged will not be able to motivate and inspire others. Yours may be a little church, but in the heart of you and your people it should be the greatest little church in the world. Forget your problems and major on the majors. Be optimistic and enthusiastic. Thank God for what you have. Sharpen up your services. Start on time. Get out on time. Fix that broken window. Act like a winner and get your chin off the ground. Your people don't want to hear about your problems; they have enough of their own. You are supposed to be a lifter, leader, and encourager. Take pride in yourself, your church, your building, your people, your work, and your Lord. Talk about your glorious past. Reiterate the victories of yesterday. Compliment your predecessors, both pastors and people. Minimize the defeats of yesterday and maximize its victories. Your church can be a winner. It will be something the people love to talk about and love to come to—all for him, all for his glory.

Christ loved the church and gave himself for it. A man likes to hear people brag on his bride. Surely our Lord is pleased when we love his church. Be proud of the building, proud of the past, proud of its victories, proud of its opportunity, and proud of its importance in the Lord's work. Make your church something that people will be proud of, and they will want to come and bring their friends. They will want others to be a part of what they have and what they are. It all starts with you, pastor. If you major on your difficulties, gripe, and whine all the while, you will develop a sour congregation and no one will want to come. The difference can be as obvious as night and day and it all starts with you.

CHAPTER 12
Smile

Jesus had the ability of attracting every segment of humanity. The old and the young alike were enchanted with the Master. Nicodemus, the Pharisee, and the woman taken in adultery, both fell under his spell. The rich young ruler and the blind beggar were equally touched with his undeniable charisma. Without question, God's Son relied totally upon his heavenly Father. The constant fulness of the indwelling Holy Spirit, and his manifestation through his own personality was the secret of his power. And yet, it manifested itself in a very warm and winsome manner. All who knew him loved him. The self-righteous and the pious were uncomfortable with Jesus, and he with them. He was genuine. He was real. Here was a genuine man who really liked people and they knew it.

When he is reproduced in our lives, we will be like him and people will like us too! They will want to be around us. They will desire to have what we have. How cold and impersonal, how dull and disinteresting are many Christians. To smile, to be sweet, to be friendly and cheery in a depressing and gloomy world is an irreplaceable part of the Christian ministry. Preacher, listen to me. If people do not like you, they will never get close enough to you to hear what you have to say. We are ambassadors of the

King. We are to point men to Christ. But if we scare them away, they will never draw close enough to be pointed. Why so many pious, sourpuss clergymen? The fruit of the Spirit is love and joy. In the Beatitudes Jesus again and again says, "Blessed are ye." Blessed means happy. Jesus came to tell people how to be happy, and let me let you in on a little secret—like pastor, like people. The church tends to take on the personality of its pastor. A stiff pastor will have a stiff church. A warm pastor will have a warm people.

A recent survey reported in the Texas Baptist paper showed that the most important factor in attracting people to a church was not in its architecture, location, parking facilities, or even the choir or the preaching. It was overwhelmingly the spirit of the church. Its warmth and friendliness and its fellowship.

The legalistic letter of the law kills. that is why so many churches are dead. But, the Spirit maketh alive and where the Spirit of the Lord is, there is liberty. And, where there is liberty, there is freedom. Where there is freedom, there is life. Where there is life, there is joy. Smile, brother, smile.

CHAPTER 13

Build a Team

As Aaron held high the hands of Moses, so our Lord has given to the fortunate pastor a wonderful staff to assist him in the work of the Kingdom. Several unalterable factors are involved in administering a staff of helpers.

1. Diversity of responsibility
2. Camaraderie
3. Respect
4. Resourcefulness
5. Dependability
6. Loyalty

A good staff member will pay for himself and then some. The wrong staff member will not only cost in uncounted difficulties and problems, but income as well. The easiest thing in the world is to hire a staff member. The hardest thing in the world is to get rid of one. Proceed slowly. The recommendation from a former area of service may be a dependable and accurate guide to his capabilities and loyalties or it may be an attempt to get rid of an incapable man. Act prayerfully, investigate carefully. The church you save may be your own!

The four most important areas involved in the beginning of the development of a new staff are:

1. Associate pastor—responsibility includes hospital work, visitation, evangelism, and uncounted details.

2. Minister of music → *Let him or her do their Responsibility.*
3. Minister of education
4. Youth director.

Depending on the size of the church and its ability to pay, various combinations of these areas of responsibility could be used. Indeed in the very small situation the first staff member could well have an area of responsibility which includes all of these. Let us review the important factors in developing and administering the church staff.

1. Set up. Clearly defined areas of responsibility should be set out in writing as a job description by pastor and people before beginning the search for a new staff member. Whether a staff is large or small, maximum efficiency will be enhanced when there is a clear-cut understanding that involves no over-lapping area of responsibility and no area of responsibility left out. A large staff can include several specialty workers in such areas as elementary education, college director, newcomer visitor, minister of evangelism, and so forth. In our staff set-up in Houston, the entire staff is under the responsibility of director of ministries, who also serves in the capacity of associate pastor. Director of ministries, associate pastor, or pastor should each have a weekly conference with each staff member to check up on progress in varied areas of responsibility and give assistance and direction to the future.

One of the newest concepts in staff responsibility lies in the use of part-time workers. Often times dedicated and talented laymen can assume responsibility in specialized areas for small, part-time salaries. The overall effect can mean far greater productivity with less total spending. Regularly scheduled planning meetings to coordinate the work of the staff are essential. A well-informed staff member, like a well-informed church member, is a happy staff member. Every situation will dictate its own particular form of staff set-up. Move slowly and prayerfully. Clearly defined areas of responsibility and authority frequently communicated can produce a smooth and productive staff relationship.

2. The staff that prays together, stays together, and the staff that plays together is a happy staff and a staff that gets things done. Believe it or not, the most common complaint I hear from staff members in other churches is that they never communicate with the pastor and do not really know him.

Every month or two, our staff and all their families gather together for a picnic or some other good form of fellowship. Every week or two we eat together. We know each other and have social as well as professional contact periodically. People know when the staff is not harmonious. A staff at outs with each other will never be able to lead a church. Building a team spirit involves knowing each other. The likes and dislikes, interests, needs, problems, and peculiarities of individuals, when understood and appreciated, like parts in a body fitting together to make a whole, will help build team spirit and build the work of the Lord.

3. Respect. As in a marriage, so in the relationship of a staff it is imperative that each member have a genuine respect for the others' talents. A lazy staff member, one

who is careless and not responsible and talks about others behind their backs, will forfeit the respect of his fellow staff members and cause disharmony. It is the responsibility of the pastor or director of ministries to solve such problems immediately. Never wait until the problem has grown to impossible proportions! Be firm but sweet. Weigh and understand the problem clearly. Handle it immediately. Disharmony resulting from unsolved problems can mean a disruption in unity and can bring about irreparable damage. It is absolutely imperative that the pastor have the respect of staff members. To do so, he himself must set the pace and lead the way. He cannot expect them to work harder than he works. He must talk with them confidently about their problems and encourage them publicly for their achievements. Mutual respect for each other is an absolute must.

4. Resourcefulness. Resourcefulness in a staff member simply means that he does not make excuses for difficulties or delay the necessary. It means that he does not run to someone else with a complaint when a small obstacle is put in his way. "The difficult we'll do right now, the impossible will take a little while" should be the theme of a resourceful staff member. A creative, responsible man will find a way. What a blessing to a pastor to know that he can give a staff member a responsibility and forget it, knowing that a mature, capable man will figure out the details, follow through, and get the job done. A staff of men who are always making excuses, never finishing their work, always doing half a job, will drive a pastor crazy and do despite to the church of the living God. Make plans,

use your brain, check up, and follow through. there is a way. It can be done.

5. Loyalty. As no plane can have but one pilot, no football team but one quarterback, no staff can have but one leader. Yet, as with the congregation, loyalty is never demanded, it is earned. the pastor should welcome the suggestions and ideas of his staff. Loyalty begins with respect. Every repeated attempt should be made to solve problems and misunderstandings between pastor and staff. In the final analysis, although the pastor may not always be right, he is the pastor and as long as the people are following his leadership, the staff must follow as well. If the time comes when a staff member can no longer continue to give him his support, then the staff member should look for another church. People vary in their opinions and approaches. That some disagree may not necessarily mean that one is wrong, but it may mean that one can serve better elsewhere than in his present situation.

It is virtually impossible for a staff with disharmony to be productive in the kingdom of God. It is equally as impossible for a group of men, bound together in common spirit and understanding to fail to enjoy the blessings of God upon their combined efforts. Honor the staff. Help them, encourage them. They are by and large good, godly, dedicated men, and the best friends a pastor ever had.

CHAPTER 14
Think Big

"As a man thinketh in his heart, so is he." It is said that big men think big and little men do not think at all. Jesus had big plans. Imagine the overwhelming awe they must have felt when he told them to go into all the world and preach the gospel to every creature. It was physically impossible. They had no ships, planes, no way to go. It was numerically impossible. They were too few. It was financially impossible. They had no money. It was legally impossible. The law forbade speaking in the name of Christ. It was socially impossible. Who would listen? And yet, he expected them to do it. How much more does he expect of us? With all of the resources that are at our disposal, is it any wonder that he said, "These things that I do shall ye do and greater." He said, "Ask anything in my name and I will do it." He thought big. He planned big. He commanded big. He expected big. The truth is that we do not plan to do big things. If you can win fifty, you can win sixty. If you can win sixty, you can win a hundred. If you can win a hundred, you can win a thousand. If you can win a thousand, you can win the world! Draw a strategy, dream a dream, plan a plan. With his help, you can do what you think you can do. Whatever you plan, whatever you invision for tomorrow, next week, next year, change it, enlarge it. No one ever did what he did not plan to do and he never planned what he did not dream. The fulfilment of the Great Commission in our generation is a possibility, but it will take big men with big dreams, willing to do a big job for a big God.

The Communists dreamed of conquering the world in 1907. In less than seventy years they are half way there. In two thousand years the Christian church only dreams and seems to be farther behind than when it started. Henry Ford dreamed of an automobile and built an empire. Campus Crusade's founder Bill Bright dreamed of taking the gospel to the world in one generation and is well on the way to its accomplishment. Jack Hyles dreamed of baptizing ten thousand converts and is well on the way. What is your dream? God is in a hurry. The world is on fire and billions are in the valley of decision. Make no little plans. Dream no little dreams. Enlarge your vision. Think big, the world is your parish.

CHAPTER 15
Set the Example

Where there is great accomplishment, there is great leadership. Real leadership does more than talk. It does. There is no substitute for hard work. When you preach on prayer, your people must know that you have prayed.

For twenty-five years, Dr. R. G. Lee led the great Bellevue Baptist Church of Memphis to become one of the world's greatest congregations. For twenty-five years the crowds came and converts were baptized every Sunday. The great man's secret in his own words—"Preach good, pray a lot, and work hard." And work hard he did! For twenty-five years, six days a week, R. G. Lee made ten soul-winning calls a day. Recently I went fishing with two men from our church. While I sat on the bank in the shade of a tree, they plugged every hole in the river for three hours. While I caught nothing, they caught twenty-seven beautiful bass. On the way back to the city I asked one of them how many times they had thrown the plug to catch those twenty-seven fish. One of them replied, "Probably about three thousand times, preacher." If you are going to catch any fish on Sunday morning, you will have to throw the plug during the week.

For five years at the First Southern Baptist Church in Del City, Oklahoma, we averaged over twenty conversions and additions every Sunday. My personal prospect visitation program was as follows. On the theory that the best prospect I will ever visit is a man who just heard me preach, I visited all Sunday afternoon every Sunday afternoon, and my staff also visited. We averaged nine conversions and additions every Sunday night for five years. Beyond Sunday it is always best to visit the prospect as near to the following Sunday as possible. A Saturday call is better than a Monday call in relation to a public Sunday morning decision. Every Monday through Thursday night I would make a couple of quick prospect calls on the way home from the office. Friday night was my major night of visitation. I would visit from 4:30 to 9:00 on Friday, and from 1:00 to 7:00 Saturday afternoons. All prospects as yet not contacted by Saturday night were then called on the telephone from 7 to 10 P.M. A telephone call is not as good as a personal visit, but it is better than nothing. In the event the prospect is not at home, leave a handwritten note stating that you were there. It too, is better than nothing. For five years I averaged thirty-five prospect calls a week and my staff another hundred or more. Our people knew we worked hard, and out of inspiration and appreciation, made an additional one thousand weekly visits. The results that came were as natural as the laws of sewing and reaping. There is no substitute for hard work.

CHAPTER 16
Walk Slowly Through the Crowds

Shortly before John F. Kennedy's fatal trip to Dallas in 1963, he was reported to have given his wife a word of instruction on meeting the many people they expected to encounter. "Dear," he said, "do not be in a hurry. Take plenty of time and give the people your undivided attention one at a time. Walk slowly through the crowds." Good advice for anyone, but particularly a preacher. As his servants, we must never but never be so interested in reaching masses of people that we give the appearance of being aloof, busy, disinterested, and generally carried away with our own importance. Jesus preached incomparable sermons to the multitudes on the mountaintop and at the seaside, but he was never better than when he preached those words to one as recorded in John, chapter three. Never act as though you are in a hurry. You can be very busy, but not give the appearance of busyness. Take time for people. Multitudes are made up of individuals with individual problems. To each, his is the most important problem in the world. When you stand in the midst of a large group of people, give them your undivided attention *one at a time* until they are through speaking to you. Better to let fifteen walk away, unwilling to wait because you were genuinely interested in one, than give partial attention to fifteen that is obviously not genuine. Take time for individuals, classes, and small groups, as well as large congregations of people. Arrive early, be relaxed, listen well. Do not be listening to one man while staring over his shoulder to see who else is watching. Be genuinely interested in the individual. Never make a grand entry. If you cannot arrive on time, then get there early, but not late.

In a busy world filled with blasting horns, flashing lights, and screaming voices, people deserve to have an island of tranquility, at least one place in the world where a little solace can be found. As God's undershepherd, you are to provide that place. An early start on the day and an extra prayer in the morning will insure the smooth flow of the day's activities and will greatly aid you in having time to be genuinely interested in other people. Don't be boisterous and make a big show of your own importance with one eye cocked to see what kind of impression you are making on the crowd. Genuine humility and sincere Christian sweetness are a rare combination in the personality of too few. Be a man of God among the people. Speak softly, look straight in their eyes. Give them warmth and genuine attention. Walk slowly through the crowds.

CHAPTER 17
Be Yourself

Preachers can be downright disgusting people. Some-one ought to write a book entitled "Games Preachers Play." The first chapter could well be entitled "Do Not Try to Act Like a Preacher." Most ministers have a pre-conceived image of how a clergyman should act, dress, walk, talk, and so forth. Trying to fit the mold and sub-scribe to the image oftentimes takes a man completely out of his own personality and into something unnatural. "I have never met a preacher that I really felt confident around or felt I could talk to," has been said too many times by laymen and laywomen. Dr. Holy Joe, Professor Bottletop, and The Right Reverend Whistlebritches can turn off more people than all the good gospel preaching can turn on.

Preaching is truth through a personality. It is God's word entrusted in human instrumentality. But, if the per-sonality turns off the hearer, they may never get beyond him to the truth he is trying to say. Do not try to fit the image. Throw away the mold. Quit playing Reverend Minister. Don't hide behind a clerical facade. Be yourself. Act natural. Act like a human being. Dress like you want to dress. Smile. Wake up. Lay off the high-sounding theo-logical phrases. Lots of you are scaring away three fourths of your potential hearers. Get the scene? It is repeated a hundred thousand times every Sunday in the hallway, on the street, and in the parking lot. The preacher greets the people with a warm and sunny "Good morning." He is cheery, natural. He is himself. But, when he walks out into the pulpit, he is someone else. He is playing his Sunday morning game. After church he is a human being again, a normal man, with a normal style, and a natural vocabulary. The people have seen him turn it on and turn it off. He tells them that religion is an everyday part of life. They are to take Christ with them everywhere. They are to be a witness in the home, in the school, and on the job. And yet, he does not do it himself. He plays the religion game for an hour on Sunday and then steps back into a world of normality the rest of the week. Everything he is, says to the man in the pew that Christianity does not cross over into the world of reality—that the bridge from Sunday to Sunday is not possible. That it is an isolated, antiquated Sunday morning charade. The preacher does not bring his religion into the world, so why should I? Can't we all play that game? And so from Sunday to Sunday, no discipleship, no witness, no nothing. The truth of the matter is that not one church in a hundred is winning anyone except the children of its own members. There is no sharp cutting edge into the world—out there in the bars and bus stations, schools and shops, stores and stadiums where the people really live. And is it any wonder? *We have scared them to death!* They are afraid if they get what we have they may become as funny as we are.

Furthermore, to emulate the preconceived universal preacher image is to frustrate the will of God. He made you like you are and put you where you are because there are more people at that time, at that place, who can relate to you, identify with you, and listen to you than anywhere else in the world. And when you try to become someone else other than you, you thwart what God is trying to do through you. Don't act like a preacher. Act like a human being. Be yourself. Do you think that there is no universal preacher image? Then you are pitifully wrong. No movie or television program ever shows a sharp, successful looking businessman-type in the role of the preacher. Never! He is always a Catholic priest; an Elmer Gantry wolf in sheep's clothing; or a hick from the sticks, a tweedledum, tweedledee, weak-kneed, watery-eyed, sissy-looking punk that is the image the world has conjured up of the preacher.

Why? Because that is the image we give. Those are the games preachers play. Throw away your backward collar, black suit, Holy Joe talk, and sour pickle look. Wake up, man. Come alive! Be yourself. Quit acting like a preacher. Someone asked me if I were a preacher. I said, "No, I have just been sick this week. That is why I look this way."

Get with it, preacher. You are scaring your congregation to death. And in case you haven't noticed, they are turning you off in droves.

CHAPTER 18
Love the People

There is a popular song which says that what the world needs is love and it needs love now. The writer of that song might have come from the local church and found it too cold, formal, empty, dull, loveless, and heartless. If Christianity is anything, it is love. Love given and love taken. Love sacrificing and love smiling. Love in action. Three thousand people in church may demonstrate love on Sunday morning and never make the newspapers. But, one act of violence and hatred makes screaming headlines. People think this is all the world really is anymore. They do not believe there is any love to be found. It is so emotionless, so heartless. Where then, is love to be found? The Bible says, "God is love," and through Jesus Christ, God lives in us. So then, the Christian is a walking island of love in a loveless world.

The visitor within your gates may not be able to explain it or define it, but he knows when it is there, and when it is not. A man will get up, dress, pass fifty other churches, and drive all the way across town if he knows that a warm experience awaits him with love and true fellowship in the house of God. And for many, it is just about the only love they will experience all week long. The church whose pastor radiates love will give love in return. Not only to him, but to all with whom they come in touch.

Give that visitor a warm handshake and a genuine welcome. Put your arm around that deacon. Tell him what a good job he is doing and how much you appreciate him. When the youth are stirred and join the church in great numbers, the old people may feel neglected. Love them. Spend time with them. Tell them you love them. Send them cards on their birthday. Ask about their children and grandchildren. Tell the people you love them. Tell them every Sunday. Thank the choir for working hard, for coming early and staying late. Walk up and down the aisles before the service. Pick up the little child, ask the kids about their peewee baseball game. Love the people, all of them. The black, the white, the rich, the poor, the lonely, and the unlovely. Herein is love. Love is not merely an emotion. Love is something you do. Jesus commanded us to love one another. He knew that you cannot command emotion but you can command action. Know your people. Mix with them. Spend time with them. Get interested in their jobs, their problems, and their promotions. Flatter them. Compliment them. Encourage them. Know what schools your teen-agers go to. Be interested in their football scores. Attend their school plays. Do not be a Sunday morning prima donna. Give love and you will get love.

Our people used to complain if they got out of church at two minutes after 12:00. Now they get out at 12:30 and still won't go home. They stand around for half an hour after church and just let the biscuits burn. They love the Lord, love the new members, and love each other. Half of the county is coming to First Baptist Church to get under the spout where the glory comes out. To love and be loved. There is something there. The spirit, the fellowship, that intangible something that makes the church alive and attracts people and holds them. What is it? It is love, man, love. Love the people.

Make your church an island of love and the world will come in droves. Every Sunday three to four hundred visitors flock to First Baptist Church, Houston. Why? LOVE, LOVE, LOVE!

CHAPTER 19
Delegate Responsibility

The President of the United States cannot do everything. He must be free to think, weigh information, and make decisions. He must have a cabinet, a group of qualified men, to inform and assist him in making and carrying out policy.

Likewise, the pastor of a growing and vibrant church must learn that he cannot be a jack-of-all-trades and make decisions and do everything himself. He must have help. The telephone and the United States Postal Services are two of the fastest and most inexpensive forms of that help. The staff, secretaries, deacons, teachers, and the membership at large all compose a large untapped reservoir of talents and abilities. Right now there is probably someone in your congregation just waiting to be asked. The elderly themselves can telephone the sick and shut-ins for you. There is a retired minister in your congregation who can help visit the hospitals. There are women to address envelopes. There are teen-agers to mow the church lawn and distribute handbills for the next revival. There are the businessmen who know how to design ads, take surveys, handle legal work, and do a hundred other things that need to be done. Do not delegate responsibility at random. The new members packet should contain, among other things, a talent survey card. Keep a master file of people's talents, hobbies, and occupations. When you need something done, go to the file. There is a mechanic who cannot teach a Sunday School lesson but can repair the church bus. There is a carpenter who cannot give great sums of money but who can build a toy chest for the children's department. There is a talented lady who can help improve the quality of the church meals. There is a groceryman who can assist in quantity ordering of foods for the weekly church dinners.

When you have a job to be done, whether it is painting a Sunday School department, follow-up of new members, or the recruitment and training of ushers for a special meeting, get a layman. Call him into your study and have a person-to-person talk. Tell him you need him. Tell him the work of the Lord needs him for a special project that only he can do. Tell him how much you are counting on him and how important he is to the work of the Kingdom. Teach him how to do what you want done. Ask him to enlist other workers, oversee the job, and carry it through, giving you a report when it is completed. Compliment him. Thank him publicly when the job is finished. Think! There is an easier way and there is probably someone that can do it. You cannot do it all, and there are a hundred good people just waiting to be asked, wanting to be used.

CHAPTER 20

Preach the Word

The Word of God is quick, powerful, and sharper than a two-edged sword. About 1967 it occured to me that I was preaching sermons about the Bible and not preaching the Bible. Topical sermons with reference to some supporting Scripture passages will not do the job. The way to build great churches and great Christians is on the whole meat of the word. Expository preaching, unfolding the Scriptures with an application for today is the only way.

Soon after I discovered the power of expository preaching, our church in Oklahoma City experienced a complete revitalization. Crowds doubled, people grew, homes were stabilized, offerings increased, and conversions went up. Periodically, organized religion seems to come up with a new absurdity. One of the latest theological jags is that we must make the gospel relevant. That, my friend, is a lot of baloney. It is not our job to make the gospel relevant. Ours is to preach it. The Holy Spirit is the one who makes it relevant. Times change, but people do not change. We have a hundred newfangled names for sin. But, sin is still sin, and the wages of sin, still death. I wonder if we need new terms for Bible words or whether we need to make our generation more familiar with the Bible words. How many times have I preached to have people say at the door, "Preacher, you must have been reading my mail this week," or, "You really talked to me this morning." I had not read their mail. I hardly knew their name. But, when I preached on one message, the Holy Spirit applied it to a thousand different needs as only he can do. I have preached on one subject and seen uncounted numbers of people solve problems of a seemingly unrelated nature because of that one message. It is Pentecost repeated. One word is preached, but people hear it in the language of their own need. This mystical power, the ability to preach one idea and have it meet a hundred different problems, is only inherent in the word of God. Topical sermons, sermons on ideas or thoughts, will certainly be accompanied by some result, but expository preaching straight out of the Scriptures will be particularly blessed. Quit trying to make the gospel relevant. You never have. You never will. You are not supposed to. It cannot be done. He will do that. You preach the word, for that and that alone he has promised to bless.

CHAPTER 21
Enjoy the Services

In an exploding suburban church and in the impossible inner-city I have found it to be the same. The hearts of people are hungry, the young and the old, the rich and poor alike. Where the services are bright and attractive, warm and powerful, that is where the people will be. Whether they drive ten blocks or ten miles, hungry people will go where there is food.

Shortly after moving to Houston, we ate at the world famous San Jacinto Inn. It was twenty-five miles from town, the roads were bad, the surroundings were dilapidated, parking was terrible, it was hard to find and hard to look at. But miracle of miracles—it was also hard to get in! The people were standing in line. The reason? The best food in the county. It does not matter where your building is, how bad your parking, or how drab the surroundings. If you are serving the product, the world will stand in line to get it.

In 1965 I stood in line for one and one-half hours in the impossible middle of New York City to go to church. The reason? Norman Vincent Peale was serving the Bread of life and the people were coming to eat!

In the city and in the suburb I have found it to be true that the Sunday morning service is your greatest evangelistic tool. A warm service, a bright and happy atmosphere, great singing, spiritually annointed preaching week after week, month after month, will draw the people. Most church services are a drag that are slow and dull, unattractive, and all done in the name of worship. Preachers say, "We have a worship service this morning and an evangelistic service at night." That's just great! Preach to the lost on Sunday night when there are none there and play high church on Sunday morning when the house is full of prospects. If you have to play high church, play Sunday night when nobody comes. I repeat, the Sunday morning service is your best evangelistic tool.

In the First Baptist Church of Houston, three hundred visitors come every Sunday morning and nearly fifty of them join every Sunday. Why? Because they like it. It is real and wholesome, bright and friendly, warm and alive. They come early and stay late. The church is difficult to find, the services are long, it is hard to park, and hard to get back to your car, but the people do not care. They do not even realize it. They like what is being served inside and they come to eat.

Wake up and warm up. Have a great, happy, vibrant, living Sunday morning service. It is the heartbeat, the life blood of everything else you do.

CHAPTER 22
Fire the Songleader

That's right! Fire him. Get him fired up and charged up or he will kill you. Long-haired music, funeral dirge anthems, and stiff-collared song leaders will kill the church faster than anything in the world. Let's set the record straight for a minute. There are no great, vibrant, soul-winning churches reaching great numbers of people, baptizing hundreds of converts, reaching the masses that have stiff music, seven-fold amens, and a steady diet of classical anthems. None. That's not a few. That's none, none, none.

Let's get the record straight on something else. We talk about a worship service on Sunday morning when what we mean is a funeral service. Worship is not necessarily synonymous with excitement and emotionalism. I am not saying that it is certainly not synonymous with quietness either, and most of us think it is. The word "worship" is an Anglo-Saxon word meaning "worth - ship," meaning the way we express our worth or place value on something. If I express my worth of a football team, an event, or situation, I get excited about it. It is the way I express my value. David got so happy with his feeling of God's worth he danced before the Lord. His enthusiasm was boundless. It could not be contained. He literally jumped with joy. You say you have a worship service on Sunday morning simply because you are quiet? They are quiet at the funeral parlor too! But, it is not because they worship, it is because they are dead! Where the spirit of the Lord is, there is liberty, warmth, life, enthusiasm, and joy. The song leader had better put some enthusiasm and life into the singing and present spiritual music that people can understand and that is as concerned with the message as with the notes. I could sight uncounted examples across the Southern Baptist Convention of what I am saying. The music should be done well. The minister of music should strive for perfection, but it is not music for music's sake which we seek. Rather, it is music for Jesus' sake, music for power's sake, and music for heart's sake.

Gerald Ray at First Baptist Church, Houston, Leroy Till at First Baptist Church, Dallas, Tommy Lane, Bellevue Baptist Church, Memphis, Bill Pearson at Travis Avenue Baptist Church, Fort Worth, and Jo Ann Shelton, a director of music for the world famous "Baptist Hour" are all perfect examples. Music with a message and music that speaks to the heart can be high quality music which can be professionally done. The gospel message need not be sacrificed for quality. There is no finer minister of music to be found on the face of the earth than our own Gerald Ray at First Baptist, Houston. He can hold his own in any group. He can conduct the *Messiah,* "Amazing Grace," or a contemporary composition, "Higher Ground," with equal finesse. But, he majors on quality music with a gospel message, well done for the Kingdom and the crowds love it and the people stand in line to hear it. I say to every music student and every dean of music that much of your music is running us into the grave. You are killing us with music to the head that ignores the heart.

Warm up, fire your hearts, fire the musicians that come through your classes. We need your help. Music is half the battle any day. Meaningless music is as out of place in a soul-winning church as a piano is at a Church of Christ convention. The world is on fire and the time is short. The minister of music can make an irreplaceable contribution to the Kingdom's work. Do not pull against us. Get with us! Help us. Face reality. High-sounding music will not win the day. To tickle the ear and ignore the heart is to ignore musical facts of the Christian life.

First Baptist Church, Houston, is a church of high-class folks. Most are college graduates and 95 percent are white-collar workers. They are educated, highly skilled, informed young adults, and nearly fifty more of them are joining every Sunday. The reason? The life style of the church—the singing, the preaching, the atmosphere, are all down-to-earth and warm. Everything about it honors Jesus and talks about him. They are not a bunch of ignoramuses that do not know good music from bad. They do. But, these young intellectuals are responding in uncounted droves to the music of the cross, the kind that speaks to the heart and needs of man.

Fire the song leader, fire the music, and you will fire the service and fire the people.

CHAPTER 23
The Invitation

There have been revivals in which some of the outstanding preachers in the world have preached to overflow audiences, night after night, with only two or three conversions. I have seen ministries in which mediocre preachers have consistently had fifty to one hundred conversions week after week. The difference? The power of the Holy Spirit, yes; preparation, yes; the power of God, yes; but I believe that the big physical difference is that all-important phase of the Christian ministry—*the ability to give an invitation.* It is a God-given gift and one that will not be learned overnight, and yet, as in most things, there are some rules to be learned. There are basic mistakes often made, which if corrected, can produce consistent results. I know of no other phase in the entire ministry of the preacher more important than drawing the net. Yet, it is at this point that most of us fail. No college or seminary courses are offered, few sermons ever preached on how to give an invitation, yet it is here that we win or lose it all. The invitation is hard.

Extending an invitation is the greatest agony in the ministry. We live and die a thousand deaths in the ten or twenty minutes in which the invitation is extended. When souls stand between life and death, we must be most dependent upon the Holy Spirit and most sensitive to his leadership. An invitation extended too long may harden some heart that can never again be touched. An invitation prematurely closed may miss that one last soul that was going to come on the next verse. Which of us feels competent to write instructions to our fellow ministers on the giving of an invitation?

I feel like the man who was dying and called a doctor. After three hours of X-rays and examination, the doctor said, "I am afraid you are going to die. Are there any last words?" "Yes," the man said, "I wish I had called another doctor."

I do not presume to tell you how to give an invitation. This must be learned in the laboratory of experience and in the school of prayer, yet there are some constant factors that should be remembered. Following are twelve suggestions that have been helpful in my own ministry at the point of extending the invitation.

1. *Give the invitation authoritatively.*—A note of authority, or the lack of it, is one of the keys to a successful ministry and one of our worst failures in giving the invitation. Set your invitation on fire and people will come and watch the fire burn. A fire must itself burn before it can give warmth to others. If *you* don't believe it, they won't believe it. Stand up on your hind legs and give the invitation with all the authority of heaven. Your frame of mind, your attitude, your approach to it all is of utmost importance. If you approach the invitation hesitantly, with a note of apology, you might as well not give it at all. Don't hesitate. Don't apologize for it—just give it! The preacher's attitude is extremely important and the man

in the pew can read your attitude. You have the authority of heaven behind you. Demand repentance, decisions, and action.

One reason we lack authority in the invitation is that we have so often heard criticism of high-pressure invitations that we go into the invitation whipped—afraid of criticism from someone. What is high pressure? I have heard a lot about it, but in fifteen years in the ministry, I have never seen any high pressure. I have never heard an evangelist tell a deathbed story; I have never heard a tearjerker. I am convinced that in most cases high pressure simply means that someone is getting the job done. If you would avoid criticism, do nothing, say nothing, and be nothing. He that would seek accomplishments and success in winning men to Christ must run the risk of the criticism of those who do nothing.

It has come to the sad state that many churches do not even give invitations anymore. May God have mercy on us. Forget what people think! You must have an authority about your ministry, especially in extending invitations, or men will not respond.

2. *Be specific.*—Never assume that your audience knows what you want them to do. A great number do not.

Several years ago a famous preacher preached an inspiring sermon on "doing something." The next day fifty men responded to the challenge, excitedly asking for something to do. The preacher confessed that he did not have anything special in mind. The fifty laymen bound themselves together to place a Bible in every hotel room in the world, and the Gideons were born.

Frequently we ask from the pulpit, Who will come for baptism, Who will come on conversion? Who will come by statement, letter, special service? The average man in the pew doesn't know letter from better, or position from profession. We must spell out exactly what it is we are asking them to do.

Some years ago an evangelist was holding a revival in Oklahoma. After three nights of preaching on communism without any kind of visible results, he moaned to the educational director, "I cannot understand why they are not coming forward." "What do you want them to do?" asked the educational director. "Come down and surrender to join the FBI?"

Explain step by step that if they are willing to change their way of life, confess their sin, put Christ as Lord and Master of their life, you want them to step out in the aisle. Explain how simple it is if they will take that first step, then the second, then the third and come to the front.

3. *Give it urgently.*—Never ask them to think it over. Never talk about tomorrow. Never refer to another chance. Jesus always called for action *today.* Immediately, tonight, on this verse, in this service, it is always now! now! now!

4. *Get into the invitation.*—The careless, unplanned manner in which many ministers and musicians make the transition from song service to message of invitation is one of the reasons for the failure of many invitations. Too often the invitation is thought of as unimportant, something to be tacked on to the end of the sermon. If you want to kill the service and the invitation, preach a splen-

did thirty-minute sermon, end on high with a thrilling illustration, and then kill it all by saying, "We shall stand and sing three verses of hymn number so-and-so, whether anyone comes or not!" Never infer that people might not come. Never be negative in an invitation. Get into the invitation without anyone's knowing it. A sharp break between sermon and invitation can destroy it all. An invitation number should never be announced. It should only be sung, softly in the background, as the invitation is extended. If you want to kill the service, finish your sermon by turning to the song leader and saying, "What is the invitation number?" You might just as well go home right there. You have lost the battle.

After the people have been looking in the evangelist's face for thirty minutes, they should immediately close their eyes and let the next image be a picture of God as they envision him. Their thought should be immediately turned to their relationship with the Lord. If, between the message and the hymn, they look at a songbook or song leader, they will be distracted.

They should never look from the face of the preacher to a page in the songbook and then close their eyes and look to God. Books should not be used by the audience in the invitation at all, except in rare instances toward the end of the invitation.

When the preacher has finished preaching, have the organist and choir primed to come in softly, humming or playing, during the last seconds of his closing illustration. This should be done by a prearranged signal from the musician. There should be no movement of any kind by the song leader on the platform until all heads are bowed.

Another possibility is that at the end of the message, the evangelist will bow his head and start praying, or he may say, "As we all bow our heads," and then keep on talking as he moves into the invitation. Or, he may or may not pray between the message and the invitation. But he should move as quickly, as smoothly, as unnoticeably as possible, from the message to having them bow their heads while the choir sings.

The opening verses should be sung only by the choir. It is nice to use a soloist occasionally on the invitation, but only toward the end of an invitation as a closing appeal.

The loud playing of the piano at the beginning of an invitation, when a smooth transition is being made, can be distracting. The opening strains of the invitation music, as the choir softly comes up in the background, should be accompanied only by the organist. It is only as the pace increases and the congregation joins in with the invitation that the piano should play. If only a piano is available, let its notes be slow and soft.

The song leader should never move his hands in the direction of the audience during an invitation. This is distracting to the audience, whose attention should be only on the minister. If the choir leader directs the choir during the invitation, let him do so with his back to the audience with gestures small and unnoticeable, standing directly in back of the evangelist. If, however, the evangelist asks the audience to sing, he should then step back, making himself almost a part of the choir, and lead the audience only with his voice. Hand directing should never be used with the audience during the invitation.

The minister and musicians should have a predetermined understanding as to who will change the invitational hymn. If the minister desires the song leader to change the song during the invitation, he should inform him ahead of time. However, because it is the evangelist who is in charge of extending the invitation, it is my opinion that he is the one that should make the changes as the invitation continues. This may be done in one of two ways. As heads are bowed, he can whisper softly to the song leader to change the invitation number. Or, the evangelist may say to the congregation, using the theme of the next hymn in his invitation, "Now as the choir begins to sing 'Almost Persuaded now to Believe,' why don't you who are almost persuaded come and make your decision tonight?" If the song leader is informed ahead of time, he can have the music ready.

It is often good, when the invitation begins to drag, for the evangelist to signal for a final two or three verses by asking everyone to stand and sing, "I Am Resolved" or "Stand Up, Stand Up for Jesus," or other militant numbers.

It would be wise for the organist, pianist, and song leader to have a list of ten invitation numbers, numbered from one to ten, so that during the invitation as the hymn is changed, the evangelist can raise up three fingers for "Just As I Am" or four for "Almost Persuaded Now to Believe," and so on. The opening invitation hymn should be the same every night and should be a hymn that is familiar. Also, it should be one that is predetermined by the evangelist and the song leader before the services begin. It should be obvious that an invitation is no place to introduce new music.

5. *Give the invitation positively.*—Never say, "If you are going to come," but, "Since you are going to come." Never say, "Will you come," but, "As you come." Never plant a negative thought. Always assume that they will come and that you expect them to come and all things are in readiness. You can help plant a positive thought in their minds. "Now you know you are going to come, you want to come, you have planned to come and now, as you do come, come quickly." It is often wise to say, "I'll meet you at the front," or, "I am leaving the platform; you leave as I do and meet me here at the altar." As they do come, take a few steps down the aisle toward them with a smile on your face, greeting them as they come. Tell them that you would be glad to come back and walk with them. Go to any length to help them to come. It is often good to say, "Make up your mind while you are still seated that you are going to come." "You came tonight because you were interested, you want to make a decision—so don't hesitate, don't delay by waiting two or three verses, but as you stand, just keep right on moving and we will meet you at the front."

Bo Baker for years has used the positive approach of urging them to stand and come forward all in one motion, saying, "You know you are going to come; as you do, we will wait for you."

In the event that no one responds to the invitation,

never scold the audience. Instead, thank God that they were there and tell the people how good it has been to be present and what a wonderful service we are going to have tomorrow night. Dismiss them on an optimistic note. Leave the service on high. Never bawl out the audience at the end of an invitation, else the next night the crowd will be down 50 percent.

6. *Give the invitation prayerfully.*—Of course, the invitation is to be bathed in great prayer. I have found in my own ministry that there is a direct relationship between the number of people who have come down the aisle and the amount of time I have spent in prayer over that particular service. Power makes people come forward in the invitation. No prayer, no power. Little prayer, little power. Much prayer, much power.

As you extend the invitation, let your heart keep talking to God. As you speak, affirm in your heart, "I believe the Holy Spirit is working. I know, dear God, that you are dealing with hearts. I believe more will come forward tonight." Pray in great faith. Expect things to happen and God will honor your faith.

7. *Give it proudly.*—In your preparation for the service, including music and preaching, plan for the invitation itself. Remember that as a representative of the King of kings, it is your holy position to extend the offer of grace to lost and dying men. It is an honor to be called from among the ranks of men to the ministry of the gospel as colaborers with Christ. Throw your shoulders back, look discerningly into the faces of the people, and urge them to receive Jesus Christ.

Make everything in the invitation the very best. Often the musicians will tend to let down. Have the choir stand proudly to their feet, look into the eyes of the conductor, and harmonize more beautifully than ever while singing the invitation hymn. Too often we carefully rehearse the special music and give little thought to the performance of the invitational hymn. Many times, Cliff Barrows will rehearse Billy Graham's crusade choirs for an hour and a half before the opening night of the crusade on "Just As I Am." Rehearse the hymn of invitation. Go over every detail of the invitation in your mind and execute it to the best of your ability.

Years ago, the first transoceanic cable message came from the king of England to the waiting hearts of millions of Americans. Seconds before the broadcast, the engineer discovered that the cable had been broken. Dramatically grasping both ends of the cable in his hands, for twenty-seven minutes the message of the king flowed through his body to the nation. In just that way, every time we stand to give an invitation, we allow ourselves to be channels through which the Spirit of Christ flows into the hearts of waiting sinners. It is a privilege to extend the invitation of the King of kings—do it proudly!

8. *Don't be afraid to give a long invitation.*—It is thrilling to see the heavens open and a flood of power come as great hosts respond on the first word of the invitation. However, it is usually true that little or no response will occur immediately and a good deal of time is often required for an invitation. While we realize that God speaks to sinners as we preach, it is often easier for him to speak

in the quietness of the invitation as we step back and let him move.

When we go into an invitation with plans to sing only two or three verses, we are saying that what we have said for thirty minutes is more important than what God may say in a minute and a half. *I have found that 90 percent of the converts come forward after the third verse of the invitation.* On a recent Sunday morning in our church, we sang nine verses without a move. This was highly unusual, but I was impressed that many were on the verge of decision. When the invitation finished, twenty-five minutes later, twenty-seven had been converted, including nine grown men.

In extending a long invitation, some variety is needed. After the invitation begins, it is often wise not to speak for three or four verses. When things begin to slow, several things can be done to keep the invitation from dragging.

(1) People may be seated and then stand again.

(2) Ask the folks to step back, that those in the middle may move to the aisle more easily.

(3) Ask Christians to speak a word of encouragement to a friend or loved one standing nearby. No one will ever be offended by a simple, "I'll go with you."

(4) Ask them to look up at you while you speak a word of encouragement and then to bow their heads again.

(5) Stop and reemphasize some point or use an illustration. In other words, let them look up at you, preach another minute or two, and then go on with the invitation.

(6) Encourage Christians to come forward and pray for friends, rededicate their lives, or join the church. Their coming may break the ice and make it easy for the unconverted to respond.

(7) Change the invitational hymn. Use a soloist for part of the invitation as you approach its conclusion. If the Holy Spirit is moving in great power and variety is used, a long invitation will not be distasteful and will prove to be very fruitful.

9. *Give a good rededication invitation.*—Never minimize the importance of rededication. Many times a rededication of life actually means more in changing the direction and purpose of a person's life than his conversion. Be specific in the rededication invitation. Spell it out.

A rededication should mean more than "I will try harder," or "I just want a closer walk with the Lord." It should mean one of two things: (1) "There are some definite things I am doing that are wrong, and I intend to stop immediately," or (2) "There are some definite things I am not doing—such as tithing, studying the Bible, witnessing, praying, attending church, and so on—that I intend to start immediately." It is that simple. In short, a rededication means that in every area of a person's life, Christ is to be given first place henceforth.

10. *Deal properly with those who come.*—Whether a person comes to join the church, be converted, or rededicate his life, the pastor or some counselor should pray with him and lead him to pray, to confess his sins to God, to dedicate his influence anew, or whatever the need may

be. I have dealt with many teen-agers and adults who went forward, saying that they had made decisions as children, but did not know what they were doing. In most cases I have found that they really did know what they were doing, but that the individual who dealt with them did not know what *he* was doing. What a tragic mistake to merely shake hands with the person, then have him fill out a card and be seated. Humble yourself, get on your knees, and deal properly with those who come, and a far greater quality of decisions will be made. By all means, don't give them a card to sign until they have prayed and their decision has been made. Do not give the card first. You may interfere with the Holy Spirit's dealings with them. Lead them quickly into their decision for Christ. The information can be recorded later.

11. *Make much of their decision.*—Too often we merely read the names of those who come: "So-and-so comes on profession of faith." "So-and-so comes on rededication." Say something about each one. Let some of them give a testimony. Shake their hands and congratulate them on their decision. Ask friends, Sunday School teachers, or parents to come and stand by them. Let them know that we believe this is a genuine experience in their life. It is a mistake to ask the church clerk to read off the names and tell the decision. There is no warmth in that. The church clerk has not led them to Christ.

Let the pastor, as shepherd of the people, present those who come, and speak a word about their decision.

Sunday by Sunday, consistently encourage the people to come by and greet those who have made decisions at the front. When 95 percent of the people head for the back door, it is like saying to the new convert: "We didn't really care whether you came or not, we were just saying that." Take time to make much of the invitation, and even more of those who have responded to it.

[Reprinted from *The Power of Positive Evangelism,* John R. Bisagno, ©Copyright, 1968, Broadman Press.]

CHAPTER 24
Inform the People

An informed people are a happy people. People will follow their pastor's leadership as long as:

1. They are confident that he is going God's way.
2. They are sure he knows where he is going.
3. They know where he is going.

The affairs and plans of the church should never be conducted under the table. Any committee meeting should be open to any interested member who desires to attend. Let the people know that you stand ready to listen to their suggestions and ideas, as well as complaints, and that they and their opinion are an important part of the policy-making of the church. No committee ever has the right to override the decision of the church or to change its policies. The people in duly constituted business sessions are the final policy-making body of the church. I have found that the committees and people will usually be only too happy to follow the leadership, plans, and wishes of the pastor if they are informed and their opinions are taken into consideration. Do not run off and leave your people. To be sure, the only way to lead someone is to get out in front of them, but don't go so fast that you leave your people. They cannot and will not follow a leader that is so far out in front of them that no contact with him is possible.

When an idea comes, write it down, pray about it, and think about it. Let the computer of your mind digest it until it is crystalized. Discuss it with your staff and polish it. Then, go to the proper committee with the suggestion of the idea. Let them assimilate it into their own thinking, improve on it at the next meeting, and present it in final form to the church. The church should not be expected to make a final judgement on a major decision at its initial presentation. Such major items as the election of new deacons, the opening of a new mission, construction of a new building, calling of a new staff member, and so forth, should be publicized well in advance with adequate information for the people. Jumped-up ideas without adequate preparation or information will give the opinion that the business affairs of the church are a railroad job by the staff and pastor. Business meetings should have ample time alloted for adequate deliberation on important issues. The pastor as moderator, must see to it that all who desire to do so, whether they be pro or con, have adequate opportunity to express themselves. When the question is called for and it is time to vote, let it be clearly understood that the majority is to rule. Give the minority the privilege of expressing themselves, listen courteously to their opinions, do not belittle them for disagreeing, but whether the vote is unanimous or only 51 percent to 49 percent, let the majority rule. Never vote twice on the same matter. Once the will of the people has been spoken, it is time to act. The fact that some committee does not agree with the previously voted action of the church, which has constituted that committee to carry out its wishes, does not matter. If a committee refuses to carry out the wishes of the church, fire the committee and get a new one. Committees and deacons do not run churches. Churches run committees and deacons. Never let the tail wag the dog!

Petty differences in secretarial staffs and staff members can arise due to differences in salaries. Every staff member or secretarial worker is not to be automatically raised because someone else is raised. Salary should be commensatory with effort, attitude, and production. Therefore, it may be wise in that particular case for the personnel committee to set salaries and for the entire salary package to be voted on as one by the church. This is one area that is the exception to the rule. However, any member of the church at any given time upon request should be given information in private regarding salary or any other matters regarding finances or policy.

Publicize activities and meetings well in advance. A church newspaper attractively done with creative artistic headings and pictures, along with Sunday morning and Sunday evening announcements printed in the bulletin and publicly repeated for emphasis, are an important tool in the matter of informing the people. Use repetition. It is amazing how many times an announcement can be made and still be missed by so many.

The old Southern spiritual says, "There is a deacon in the church, but he don't deac right. Tell me, what we gonna do? Everybody pull together, let the church roll on! There is a woman in the church and she talks too much. Tell me, what we gonna do? Everybody pull together, let the church roll on. There is a singer in the choir and he don't sing right. Tell me, what we gonna do? Everybody pull together, let the church roll on."

The people of God can be trusted. They can always be counted on to make the right decisions regardless of the opposition of the few when adequately informed and spiritually enlightened. As you lead them under God, be sure that you take them with you. Leadership is never demanded, it is earned. If the people are convinced that you know where you are going and they know where you are going, and together you are going where God is going, they will follow your leadership. *But they must know.* Through the proper channels, through the church paper, and through the church services, inform the people.

CHAPTER 25
Appoint Committees

Of the many forms of church government, the democratic process of the rule of the majority is the finest. Before the baptism of the converts, Peter asked the entire congregation, "Can any man forbid water seeing that these have received the Holy Ghost as well as we?" The democratic form of church government is in accordance with the New Testament. Much preliminary work can be eliminated, however, through committee action before most matters are presented to the people for final approval. Proper use of the committee system can virtually eliminate every church problem and insure the harmonious on-going process of the work of the Kingdom.

In seven years of pastoring Baptist churches, I have never had a fight in a business meeting or ever had a major conflict on the floor of the church. There have been minority votes, but the minority has been given the right to speak and their opinion carefully listened to with the foregone conclusion that regardless of the vote, everyone would happily abide by the will of the majority. *I have not always had my way, but I have always been willing to abide by the will of the majority.* The committee system has, in my opinion, been the major contributing factor to the smoothness and efficiency of the church business. It is of absolute and imperative importance that positive, forward-thinking, sweet-spirited cooperative people be placed on committees. Like it or not, we must admit that there are some persons whose basic tendencies are to be negative, critical, pessimistic, and against everything. Some men see a glass half full. Others see that same glass half empty. Give me a committee member who sees it half full, who dares to say "can do," who looks for the bright side, for without a vision the committee, like the people, will perish.

The committee member with a constant record of pessimism and negative thinking should be replaced. The work of the church is to be done in faith and *it is to be done!* It must go on! A church is not a business and cannot be run like a business. It does not operate on dollars and cents, profit and loss basis, and the man whose mind does not think in channels of faith, who does not see beyond the realities of today into the hope of the future, has no business serving in a place of responsibility in the church. How then, are we to assure that spiritual, positive, informed, forward-thinking people be placed on committees?

1. They are not to be appointed by the deacons. The deacons are not leaders of the church, they are servants of the church.

2. It is not best to allow nominations from the floor of the church. It is laboriously impossible to do so.

3. They are to be appointed by a committee on committees, a hand-picked group of five or six, who are in sympathy with and knowledgeable of the on-going plans and desires of the pastor and people. This committee can be appointed by the church, by last-year's committee on

committees, or by the pastor. But, by all means, it should be 100 percent in sympathy with the programs and wishes of pastor and people. I have found that a sweet-spirited committee on committees is only too happy to work with the pastor. They should be particularly careful in working with him in the selection of a few of the major committees such as personnel, finance, and missions, with whom he will work closely all year long. How absurd to insist that the President of the United States work with the cabinet that he does not like, did not want, did not help select, and that is not in agreement with what he is trying to do. Give the pastor a cabinet he can work with. Any church worth its salt should do at least that much for him.

While there are certain basic committees which are common to all churches, there are certain committees that are peculiar to some. The First Baptist Church, Houston, has an elevator committee and an inner-city ministry committee. Most suburban churches would not need such committees. When matters arise which call for a particular study group to deal with a particular matter unrelated to any other existing committee, work with your committee on committees, and appoint an entirely new committee.

When you begin a bus ministry, it will be necessary to create a bus committee. If you create a recreational program, it will be necessary to create a parallel recreation committee. In accordance with your church's policy, your committee may report directly to the church, or to the deacon body and then to the church. By no means should any committee answer to another committee. The following guidelines should be used in the appointment of committees.

1. Have adequate committees for the churches' ministry.

2. Blend a good balance of new members and long-time members, young people and old people on committees.

3. No one should be on two committees at once.

4. No one should be chairman of a committee over two years in a row.

5. At least half of the members of any committee should be new each year.

6. Unfaithful committee members should be replaced with ones who will serve.

7. Committees should not meet without knowledge of the pastor and without giving him a schedule of matters to be discussed to give him an opportunity to inform them of his opinion on the issues.

8. All committee chairmen or secretaries should give monthly written reports to the pastor. It is well for the pastor to meet with committees whenever possible, but not necessarily every meeting. A committee should always inform the pastor of decisions made in his absence and should never bring recommendations to the deacons or floor of the church without his prior knowledge. Express appreciation to faithful committee members for a job well done. Have a prearranged agenda, stay on the point, listen to their opinions, and the committee system can be a lifesaver to the program of the pastor and the church.

CHAPTER 26

Love the Deacons

The New Testament office of deacon is not one of leadership, it is one of service; it is not for making policy for the church, but for carrying out the policies of the church; not telling the church what to do, but doing what the church tells them to do. It is unfortunate that in many instances they have become the board of directors, the governors of the church. *This ought not to be.* Suggest that your church rename the deacons to "deacon body" rather than deacon board. Preach on the qualifications of the deacon. Remind deacons and congregation that they are the servants of the church and express your appreciation to them for services rendered. I have found that most deacons really would not have it any other way and that in reality they are only too happy to assume the proper New Testament role of service rather than leadership in the church. By and large, we have forced them into a role of policymaking and leadership which they neither want nor have sought.

After nearly twenty years in the ministry, I have found some very enlightening facts about churches.

1. Most of the churches that have serious problems are in the area of a deacon-pastor conflict.

2. Most of the conflict is at the point of deacons attempting to follow the unscriptural practice of running

the church.

3. Most of the time the problem would never have arisen had not the proper New Testament order of pastor-people-deacon been altered.

4. Most deacons really do not want the role of leadership. It has been cast upon them by tradition and by members unwilling to fulfil their responsibility.

5. Most deacons are godly and spiritual men who would be only too happy to serve the church and follow the pastor if he is a strong and competent leader, an apparent man of God, and kind and appreciative of their individuality and role of responsibility. You will attract a lot more flies with sugar than with salt. Too many preachers approach a new pastorate with a chip on their shoulder expecting to find conflict with the deacons, and they are not disappointed.

Listen to that deacon. Understand him. Love him. In most cases, you will find him to be genuinely God's man. A man that loves the Lord and his church and is only too happy to pray and to serve does not have to be a deacon. He does not have to come to church every time the doors are open. He does not have to take time from his busy schedule to serve. Act like you love him. Pray for him. Express your appreciation. Commend him publicly. Love him and he will love you in return and your Lord through you. The men that have helped me the most in my pastorates, who have contributed most to my own spiritual welfare and that of my church, have been my deacons. I love and honor them and they do me in return.

CHAPTER 27
Raise the Budget

People like to be identified with success. They like to follow the crowds, to be "where it's at." Everybody likes a winner. When the Yankees are winning, the stadium is packed. When they are losing, very few come. When great crowds are attending the church, the momentum brings even greater crowds. It is easier to raise an offering for a successful evangelist wearing a new suit than a poor missionary with holes in his shoes. I am not suggesting that it should be that way, I am stating one of the facts of life. So? Simply this. Set your budget high. Knock the top out. Put on a first-class stewardship campaign. Do some big thinking. Get the people thinking big. They like to be identified with that.

Scores of my men used to give more money to other church organizations than to our church. I could hardly blame them. Other organizations were winning thousands. We were winning very few. But, now it is different and they are giving their money through the church. That is as it should be. Set a good budget with a challenging increase and make every attempt to subscribe it. Remember five things:

1. Involve the people.
2. Make a challenging budget.
3. Inform the people of God's plan for meeting the

budget.

4. Give them opportunity to make their pledge to the budget.

5. Remind them repeatedly to pay those pledges.

You cannot bargain out of a position of defeat. People will not give weekly because you harrass them endlessly about being behind on your bills. They will give because your church is successfully and consistently paying its bills. *Remember that principle.* You cannot raise money for a dead horse. They will give from victory quicker than from defeat, because you are paying your bills rather than because you cannot pay your bills. If you have a financial pledge campaign, which you should have every fall, and announce victory, the people will want to be a part and gladly pay those pledges and then some. If the pledge campaign fails, you will create an atmosphere of despair which will not help create an incentive to give. *A successful stewardship campaign is a must.* Let us review those four steps necessary to a successful budget subscription.

1. *Involve the people.*—Three months, two months, and one month in advance inform every organization head and committee head that budget preparation time is near. Tell them to have numerous planning meetings and present their budget requests by September 1. Encourage all church members to send written suggestions to the budget planning committee with individual ideas for changes in the new budget.

2. *Challenge the people.*—Begin challenging the people early in light of the promises of God, increased world responsibility, the blessings of God, increase local and

worldwide need, increase cost of living, and the necessity of evangelism in light of the soon return of our Lord. The only way to fly is a sizable increase in the budget. Challenge them to do more, much more this year than the past.

3. *Inform them of God's plan for meeting the budget.* —Bingo parties, cake walks, rummage sales, and car washes are not God's way of financing the kingdom. The tithe is the Lord's. It is holy unto him. Tithes and offerings are God's plan. I have never seen a man get mad because he was told in the spirit of love that the Bible said the tithe belonged to God. Freewill offerings may be given over and above to Christian organizations, but the tithe belongs to the Lord through the local New Testament church. They are to be laid aside consistently on the first day of the week. There, in the local New Testament congregation, the tithe must be brought.

4. *A stewardship campaign.*—Early in September the budget committee should go to work. By the first of October it should be complete. It should be presented well in advance, and voted on by the people the first of November. The month of November is to be spent in a stewardship campaign. This will consist of sermons, testimonies, and devotionals, Sunday School lessons, posters, dinners, goals, and slogans informing the people of the challenge and blessing of tithing, and of the church budget needs. On the first of December, pledge cards are to be mailed out to all the members. Two or three follow-up letters should follow. All pledge cards should be in by Christmas. Christmas week total budget subscription is arrived at in

the following manner.

—Total the pledge cards

—Add what the present membership gave last year that did not sign pledge cards.

—Add the two together and you have the total amount subscribed.

Overall, a man's former giving record, though he does not sign a pledge card, will be a more accurate gauge of his anticipated giving than a signed card. Announce the total subscribed amount the last Sunday of the year and begin operating on the new budget January 1.

5. *Repeatedly remind the people to pay those pledges.* —Letters, announcements, and sermons on faithfulness throughout the year will be necessary. Remind the people that the church does not pay her bills once a year or once a month, but weekly. The tithes and offerings are to be brought, not sent, when possible, and they are to be made consistently on the first day of the week. Consistency in giving is a must. To spend an entire year enjoying the fact that the budget has been subscribed is one of the healthiest factors in contributing to a wholesome atmosphere that is conducive to financial success. Be creative, organize well, involve your laymen, and approach it as a happy, victorious event, and you can subscribe your budget and keep financial pressure off the church and give priorities to evangelism.

CHAPTER 28
Get Out of That Rut

Get this straight. The gospel does not change. The message does not change, but the way we get out the message must be as up-to-date as tomorrow's newspaper. Preaching to the masses or teaching the individual is still God's way. He has chosen the foolishness of preaching to save them that believe. It is neither antiquated nor irrelevant. But, the way we preach, the way we teach, and the way we communicate must be as subject to change as TV preaching is removed from circuit riding preachers. Change the order of service. Take the offering last. Change visitation from Monday to Friday. Have a revival in a tent. Cancel mid-week services Christmas week. Walk out into the crowd and shake hands with the people before church. Do something different. Have a "Jesus March." Have an all-church picnic. Have a staff softball game. Create catchy newspaper ads. Preach a five-minute sermon. Have a drama on Sunday morning. Use three choirs together instead of one. Think man! Do something different. You may be boring your people to death.

For twenty years I have been preaching that I would like to see one revival in which people got as excited for Jesus as they do for a little ten-inch pigskin at a football game. And then it happened! We had just such a revival with evangelist Richard Hogue. Oh yes, it scared some of our people to death, and thank God, I hope they never get over it! Uncounted thousands of teen-agers were turned on to Jesus. How they applauded, how excited they were, and how refreshing to see. They cheered and applauded at the name of Jesus. They cheered at the announcements. They cheered at the offering. They cheered at the baptism. They knocked down the doors. They clamored to get in.

We talk about getting out of the rut, but do we really want to? Fire burns up everything that gets in its way. When revival fires spread like a prairie conflagration, they make some changes. We preach revival, we talk revival, but do we really want revival? Most churches want a revival, but they don't want one that will change anything. They talk about getting back to normal after the revival. Baloney! Normality has been killing us. Change is hard. Change does not come easy, but revival means change. When revival comes and things change, take the people as far as they will go with the revival. But, if a cantankerous few do not like the change and want to go back to their normal nothing, forget them. Run over them. But, let the revival go on. In God's name, man, let it go!

CHAPTER 29

Publicize the Church

People will not go to a place, attend an activity, or buy a product they do not know exists. The importance of good publicity cannot be overstated.

The first Christmas angel publicized tidings of good peace. The two-by-two, person-to-person witnessing taught by our Lord cannot be improved upon. But, it is not inconsistent with the principle of mass publicity. The two go hand in hand. As the B-52 bombers soften up the terrain for the foot soldiers, so publicizing through the mass media helps to climatize an area making it easier for one-by-one personal witnessing and invitation. "Oh yes, I have heard of that church. I'll try to come sometime" is a lot more likely to be heard than "where's that again?" when you publicize.

Bumper strips do little good. They are too small and move too fast. If they are to be used, only one or two words should be printed. Attractive wrought iron signs in church members' yards are helpful. Radio spots not to exceed ten or fifteen seconds and with repeated exposure are good. Don't quote Scripture passages. don't preach sermons in spots. Take a few seconds, get to the point, and move on. Billboards are good. They should be lighted, on major freeways, on the right side of the road, and not cluttered with too many words. Any handbills, invitations, or advertisements should be done professionally. Do not pass out junky homemade mimeographed invitations to anything. Do it first class. Most newspapers and radio stations will carry announcements about your churches' upcoming activities when neatly typed, well-written, concise reports are mailed to them well in advance.

Good newspaper ads should contain pictures and plenty of white space. Again, do not clutter. Get to the point and always specify a right-hand page location in the main news section when submitting advertising.

Creative TV advertising is tops but usually prohibitive due to cost. A live Sunday morning radio broadcast is a great help, and live TV can be even better. Live TV broadcasts will not hurt your church attendance. If you offer a good product, it will ultimately enhance it.

Get a slogan. No one lives near our church. We are in the heart of the inner-city, several miles from any homes. We operate on the theory that we must offer the "plus" to get the added difference of attendance. Our slogan, "It's worth a trip to town," bespeaks everything we try to do. Have a slogan that is justified and have one that does not belittle any other church or even belittle yourself. "Come, help us grow" or "The littlest church in the city" may not have such a good public effect after all. Make it truthful and make it positive.

Major on your assets. Do not advertise your problems. Do not expect an advertisement to pay off immediately. Advertising in cooperation with many other factors, however, will ultimately produce the desired effect for your church.

CHAPTER 30
Buy a Bus

The most exciting new tool of evangelistic outreach is the church bus ministry. Nothing, I repeat, nothing will increase attendance, increase converts, and increase motivation of the people as fast. Unbelievable stories from all across America and from all denominations have come regarding the miraculous growth of churches using this vehicle. How do you start?

1. Appoint a bus committee.

2. Check out what others are doing. Jack Hyles "Church Bus Handbook" is a good source. The Home Mission Board of the Southern Baptist Convention has recently compiled information regarding church ministry as well. Consult other pastors for firsthand information.

3. Sell your people. Invite a respected pastor who has had success in the bus ministry to preach to your people on this subject.

4. Make a survey. Determine by door-to-door survey and area analysis the best areas in which to begin a bus route. In our own church, we have found the door-to-door neighborhood plan to be less effective than running buses to concentrations of people such as trailer parks, apartment complexes, girls' and boys' homes, military institutes, low income housing areas, and so forth. The Brotherhood and WMU, the RA's and Acteens can put genuine

mission desire into action here. Unsaved boys, girls, men, and women of every kind and color are probably within the mission field area of your church. Find them and bring them in.

5. Buy a bus. For very little investment one or two buses may easily be purchased. Do not buy six- or eight-thousand dollar buses. Good buses can easily be chartered for occasional out-of-state trips. The ordinary Sunday run, however, will normally be less than fifteen miles per week. Used buses in the $300 to $500 category with good, safe brakes, steering mechanism, and tires will be more than adequate for Sunday morning work. They should be painted some color other than school bus yellow. Men in your church can probably handle painting and minor repairs. Maintenance, gasoline, and insurance can become expensive but will still be less expensive in the long run than leasing the buses.

6. Enlist workers. Let me be very frank and say that it takes a certain kind of dedicated Christian layman to be willing to serve in the church bus ministry. Six hours of Saturday visitation weekly is a must. It would not be possible in these brief pages to give detailed instructions for a bus ministry. Adequate information is available through other books. In general, however, you will need a bus driver, a bus captain and his wife to be bus hosts on their bus. These, along with a dedicated group of helpers must visit their routes weekly, help the children on and off the bus, keep order, keep records, follow up the parents, and either sit with the children in church or be in children's church.

CHAPTER 31
Write It Down

It would not be possible for me to overemphasize the importance of creative thinking. The things that we have not done, the tools we have not used in the work of the Kingdom are unlimited. You can develop a mind that is open to new thoughts and ideas from the Spirit of God if you try. Think. Always think.

Twenty-four hours a day I am never more than a few inches away from a note pad and pencil. Write down every idea you have. Write down suggestions for your staff, ways to improve the services, calls that need to be made. Keep a list of things to do and do them at your earliest convenience. The importance of writing down ideas when they come cannot be overstated. It is twofold.

1. Regardless of how good your memory is, you will forget things if you do not write them down. Although they may not be the most important thing you will do, they will, however, be of some importance, as one idea will suggest another.

2. By writing down every idea as it comes, you keep your mind open and receptive to other new ideas that might come. The mind, then, is not so cluttered with one hundred ideas that the new one cannot enter. Scientists tell us that we probably never use over 10 percent of our learning capacity. What a shame that so much potential

is wasted. The mind is like a computer. After a period of time, the subconscious mind will produce good ideas, but only as a result of other ideas that have been fed into it. Talk, listen, think, observe. Read about life, God, the world, progress, and the church. Read about everything. We can learn much by listening and assimilating materials, by allowing them to ferment in the subconscious mind, and using the resulting ideas. Assimilate knowledge and ideas from every possible source. Keep your mind open to the ideas that come and write them down as they do. That fleeting thought may be a gold mine of spiritual force in the Kingdom. But, by all means, write it down when it comes so that your mind is constantly clear and open.

CHAPTER 32
Act on Faith

I have stated previously that the church is not a business and it does not operate on the same principles as a business. Indeed, such is the entire premise of the kingdom of heaven. By faith, Abraham moved. By faith, Jacob offered. By faith, Moses followed. Our religion is not called the Christian faith for nothing! *Without faith, it is impossible to please him.* People must repeatedly be taught that the principles that are operative in the kingdom of God are not the same as those at work anywhere else in the world. One plus one does not always make two in the Kingdom. Ten minus one is not always nine. It is more likely to be eleven, twelve, or fifteen. Tithing does not take away. It adds. Physical necessities of life, food, clothing, and shelter are not to be found by seeking them, but by seeking first the kingdom of God. It is difficult for most church members to live in a cold, hard, success-oriented materialistic world all week, and move into a world of faith on Sunday. Oftentimes God places obstacles in our way to see how we will respond. He did not want Abraham to sacrifice Isaac. He wanted him to be willing to.

A church has no business keeping money in the bank, saving for a rainy day! The best defense is a good offense. Get that money out of the bank and into circulation. Put it to winning souls. The people of God did not give it to the church to hoard, but to minister. A man says, "We cannot advance, we cannot put on new staff members and initiate new programs because the attendance is going down." Man, this the very reason you must act on faith. Do what you cannot do, but must do! God honors faith!

CHAPTER 33
Baptize the Converts

Baptism has no part in salvation, but I seriously doubt the genuineness of the profession of faith of a man who refuses to be baptized. Baptism is the first step in obedience to Christ. If salvation is anything, it is that. A commitment to a life of obedience and discipline to the Master.

As one would help a newborn child in learning to take its first step, so it is essential to help the new convert in taking this first step of obedience. Everything should be done to facilitate his baptism. Every effort made to bring it about as quickly and easily as possible. How often have I marveled at a pastor who merely announces on the closing Sunday morning of a revival, "All who have been saved and desire to be baptized, please come to my office tonight at 6:00." One reason we baptize so many of our converts in Houston is that we try to do so. We make every effort. We work at the job. We go into every home immediately and talk to the parents of children and teenagers about their baptism. Attempts are made to arrange for their baptism at the very next service. All adults are asked to be baptized at the next service. We do not apologize for telling people they need to be saved nor should we hesitate to tell them that they should be baptized, to tithe, to serve the Lord faithfully in his church, and to search the Scriptures and pray. Make every immediate effort in the home of all of the converts to baptize them at the next service.

Keep a thorough list of all the converts. When they are baptized, they will go into the membership files. As long as they remain unbaptized, repeated visits should be made monthly until they are either baptized or until a final no is given.

The baptistry at the First Baptist Church of Houston is never emptied except to be cleaned and is refilled immediately. Every Sunday night, Sunday morning, and Wednesday night we are always ready to baptize those who are saved. Our converts receive three counseling sessions: (1) At the time they are saved, (2) Back in the home immediately, and (3) The evening they are baptized.

All of the converts from the Sunday evening service and Wednesday evening service are to meet forty-five minutes before the next Sunday morning service in the pastor's office for a final pre-baptism session. All of the converts from the Sunday morning service meet forty-five minutes before the evening service. After these three counseling sessions, the people are baptized. In the final counseling session, give instructions as to the meaning of baptism, location of the dressing areas, and so forth.

As the first step of obedience, baptism is important. If the new Christian is not helped to walk through this first step of obedience, it will be very difficult for him to take continued steps. Make the first step in the growth process as easy as possible.

CHAPTER 34
Follow Up New Members

To take new members in the front door is one thing. To keep them from going out the back door is quite another. That they "dip 'em and drop 'em" ought not and should not be said of any church. The total process of evangelism is never complete until the evangelized themselves become evangelists. The conservation of the converts is of utmost importance.

For five years First Southern Baptist Church of Del City, Oklahoma, was one of the fastest growing churches in the world. Her critics assumed that quantity implies necessity to forego quality. But, such was not the case. During the four months interim when the church was pastorless after I moved, attendance, conversions, and income all increased. Today, under the incomparable leadership of her dynamic young pastor, James T. Draper, the church continues to break every existing record. "Quality and quantity are possible."

During the first twelve months in Houston in addition to hundreds of other individuals, 150 entire family units, mothers, fathers, and children joined the church. On my first anniversary a survey showed that eight families had moved out of town, seven had become ministers of music or pastors of other churches, and exactly 135 of the remaining 135 were still faithful.

Building a great church means building great people. It involves making disciples of converts and spiritual men of boys. Our follow-up program consists of the following:

1. A biannual membership survey to check up on our people to know who they are, where they are, and how they are.

2. The new converts must be well-born in the Kingdom. They must not be allowed to abort at this delicate moment of spiritual birth. Make much over each one as they are presented to the church. Insist that the membership receive and welcome them individually. Take time to learn the names of each. A new-member indoctrination room should be arranged near the auditorium. A private after-church meeting in the new member's room should include introduction of staff, get-acquainted time, and explanation of new members packet contents.

3. A deacon's follow-up program. Every new family is assigned to a deacon. Their spiritual welfare is his responsibility. He is to visit them in the home the week they join, make a second visit a week later, a third visit a month later, and a fourth six months later.

4. All new members should be told that they are being automatically enrolled in Sunday School and Training Union. Their name is entered into the Sunday School and Training Union register Monday morning and immediately mailed to a teacher and director.

5. A new members' class taught by the pastor, associate pastor, or qualified layman is conducted on a revolving basis for thirteen weeks during the evening training hour. Membership is automatic and attendance is expected.

CHAPTER 35
Minister to the People

One of the subtle temptations of an ever-expanding pastorate is to become so involved with the matters of growth that the individual needs of the people are neglected. Counseling, weddings, hospital calls, funerals, and church socials constitute most of the needed areas for personal attention. While it is well for our people to know that we are busy about the Lord's work and are not asking them to do what we do not do ourselves, we must never give them the image of being too busy for them.

While a church member is undergoing the crisis of the death of a loved one, they do not particularly care about last week's attendance or next week's financial drive. All they care about is their personal need, and well they should. Never be too busy with the responsibility of the whole to gladly pause and give individual attention to the needs of your people.

One of the most difficult areas of ministry is the funeral. No college or seminary course and certainly no chapter in a book could aptly relate the "how to" for a pastor. As one must learn to swim by swimming, so there is no substitute in caring for the needs of the bereaved than to learn by doing. The best plan in my experience, however, is to make an immediate call to the home upon hearing of the death. It is well to leave some comforting words of printed material at that time. If the family is not home on the initial visit, a note should be left on the door and every attempt made to find the people at the cemetery, funeral parlor, or home of one of the relatives. If this is not effective, hourly calls should be made by a secretary until they are located. After the people have been located and the initial contact made in person, a second call on the telephone should be made late that night, reassuring the family of your interest and careful preparation for the funeral service. The day of the funeral, visit the home again and have prayer with the family prior to the service. It will be well to personally meet each of the other relatives who have gathered at that time. It is important to be seated on the platform before the services before the family enters so as not to give the appearance of having rushed in at the last minute. Stand by the casket at the end of the service as long as the family desires to remain. A gentle word, a sympathetic touch, a last comforting prayer can be of great benefit at this time. After the funeral, it is well to make a final evening call in the home. It is at this point that the family will be more relaxed and eager to express their appreciation. While it is not particularly necessary for *you* to hear their expressions of gratitude, it is of great therapeutic value to *them* to be able to do so. In addition, a call a week or two later is most helpful.

Weddings are happy times and should be entered into seriously, but with great joy. Once again, it is important not to give the impression of being hurried. Arrange a premarital counseling session for the couple ahead of time. The night of the wedding rehearsal should be completely relaxed. The entire wedding party should be seated at the front of the auditorium and the evening begun with a casual explanation of what is to follow. Assure the people that it is not greatly involved and there is nothing about which to be nervous. Rather, that the entire ceremony is really very simple and that you will be guiding them step by step. Personalize the ceremony. Many young couples will want to make a tape recording of the ceremony. Say something personal in each ceremony that will cause them to remember when listening to the tape many years later that it was particularly for their wedding. Make some reference to how they met or what their parents or church have meant to them. A post-wedding call four to six weeks later in the home reassuring them of your continued interest can contribute much to your future relationship as their pastor.

If time will possibly permit, hospital calls should be made as much as possible to be timed with the convenience of your schedule and that of the hospital. People will hardly appreciate a call at 6:30 A.M. when they are barely awake and have had little opportunity to prepare for the day. As in the funeral call and the wedding counseling and rehearsal situation, prayer is always appropriate. When you cannot go yourself, a staff member or deacon should always be instructed to say, "The pastor asked me to come for him. He is interested and praying for you."

A distraught caller on the other end of the telephone, wanting someone to come right away, can often be calmed and counseled by a prolonged telephone conversation. While we are always to be accessible to our people in times of need, often a late night call can be handled simply by listening at length. After the caller has had ample opportunity to talk out his dilemma, it may be easy for him to see that tomorrow will be adequate time for a personal counseling session. Counseling carefully, not only with children, but with teen-agers and adults as well, will keep many problems from arising in the future.

In counseling sessions, hospital calls, and death calls, the most important thing is not what you say, but simply that you listen. The fact that you cared enough to be there says more than a hundred words of theology and comfort. Jesus turned aside again and again from the press of the great congregations to give pastoral attention to the needs of the individual. Let us, as undershepherds, do as much.

CHAPTER 36
Have a Bible School

Through the years Bible School has been one of our great instruments of outreach. Let us get something straight. According to the 1968 edition of the Southern Baptist *Quarterly Review* the leading churches in baptisms baptized a lower percentage of children than did the churches baptizing smaller numbers. The great evangelical churches of the world are not baptizing mostly children. While I believe that children can be saved, I am not suggesting that we raid the children's departments to pad the baptism statistics. Bible School can be a time of winning some of the older boys and girls to Christ that are ready to be saved. But, it can be an equally important time of influencing brothers and sisters, neighbors, and parents with the gospel message. It is also an intensified season of seed planting for future harvests. Bible School should be a happy time. It is a time for pastor, workers, and children to work and play, to share and grow together, and have a wonderful experience in the Lord. I have grown closer to the children in my churches during the two weeks of Bible School than the entire rest of the year combined. Here are some good Bible School tips.

1. Plan well in advance. Select workers early. Increase their vision. Order the materials. Enlarge the organization. Make no little plans for Bible School.

2. Expect to do more this year than last. Increase the organization by at least 20 percent and expect to reach it.

3. Get only workers that are sweet, happy, and genuinely enjoy working with children.

4. Have a parade. Whether you are in the inner-city, suburbs, small town, or the country, get buses, cars, decorated bicycles, dogs, pet coons, and so forth. Get everyone and everything and have a parade. Some people will be attracted and come. But, the primary benefit of a parade is to be realized from the enthusiasm of the participants themselves.

5. Have an adequate break for play and refreshments in the middle of the learning sessions.

6. Give awards as incentives for daily attendance.

7. Circulate daily from room to room and associate with the children.

8. Enlist Intermediates and young people if not to attend, to at least work helping children across the street, opening doors, sponsoring games, etc.

9. Have a picnic. Point the last week toward a climactic all-school picnic with games, food, and fun for the children.

10. Tell the Bible story yourself. You need not necessarily follow the prescribed stories. A ten-message series can be brought on men of the Old Testament, men of the New Testament, the Ten Commandments, the ten great questions of the Bible, the ten great themes of the Bible, the ten great promises of the Bible, the ten great events of the Bible, etc.

11. Have a two week Bible School. Have a bright, happy atmosphere. It is really no more difficult than to have one week. Twice as much good will be done and twice as many will be saved. You miss a great blessing if you do not have a two week Bible School.

12. Give an invitation every day. By giving a very brief, low key, emotionless, pressureless, daily invitation, two benefits will accrue:

(1) The results will be scattered. Three or four coming each day instead of fifty the last day will help to insure a greater quality decision with less likelihood that some would come because others do.

(2) It is easier to follow up on the decisions in the homes every night with a smaller number of decisions recorded.

Bible School should rank with annual enlargement campaigns and revivals as priority outreach opportunities. Clear the calendar and plan well in advance. It should be no little item on the church calendar. It is one of your great tools of outreach.

CHAPTER 37

Have a Rally

A one-, two-, three-, or even five-night evangelism rally can often reap the same results as a week-long meeting without the usual accompanying cost in financing and time. Some year, instead of planning a two week long revival, plan six weekend revivals, or twelve one-night revivals. There is nothing particularly sacred about a seven- or eight-day revival. Variations can be most beneficial. It is easier to motivate and mobilize the people to point toward one big night than seven. It is also often easier to secure the desired speaker on a one-night basis. Unless the speaker is well known and has wide public appeal, general publicity will benefit little for a one-night rally. The personal approach is better here. Assign the prospects to individuals. Write and contact them personally. On any given night you could have a simultaneous hot-dog party for the kids and a prospect supper for the adults. Oftentimes a hundred prospects can easily be gathered for one night to hear an outstanding speaker.

Try a departmental revival. Use the fellowship hall instead of the auditorium. Bring all of the Juniors together on Monday night, teen-agers on Tuesday, the entire church during the prayer meeting on Wednesday, young adults on Thursday, and senior citizens on Friday. Plan a dinner, program, and speaker appropriate to each group on a one night each basis. You can reap the usual effects of a full-fledged week-long revival and no one be expected to attend over one night. At least four or five times a year bring in an outstanding personality for one night. The mechanics are really very simple. Book the man in advance. That night, personally enlist prospects, take an offering, preach, and give an invitation. The overall effect can be as refreshing as an entire week of services and much less costly and demanding of the people. Normally the most successful night for a one-night rally will be a Monday. People tend to forget. Something announced, reminded, and promoted on Sunday will be more easily remembered on Monday than the following Friday. That outstanding speaker who would be unavailable for a week is often available for a one-night rally. All the way around, it can be a most rewarding experience.

At this time, we have the names of one thousand prospect families who have attended our church in the past six months and have not joined. Our next revival will be called "Operation Inreach" with no outside publicity or effort to enlist the general public at large. Every effort will be made to reach those within. They will be contacted specifically and personally with an attempt to reach them. Bring those prospect files up to date! *And don't tell me you do not have any prospects!* Unless you are the only man living on a desert island, you have prospects. They may not be the kind of prospects you are used to reaching, but they are there.

CHAPTER 38
Get Exposure

As the big bombers soften up the terrain to make the enemy vulnerable to the ground troops, mass publicity creates community consciousness of your church. In this atmosphere it is easier for your people to witness and to bring folks to your church.

Our Lord has said, "If I be lifted up from the earth, I will draw all men unto myself." Without question, it is the drawing power of Christ that wins men. He has, however, entrusted that ministry into earthen vessels, and the more people know about you, the greater possibility of their coming to your church to give you the opportunity to exhalt the Lord. Let your people know that you are interested in speaking to civic clubs, conventions, banquets, PTA meetings, and other secular groups. Be well informed on your assigned subject without preaching at them. Make a spiritual application. Make sure that your statistics are correct. Stay within the time limit. Omit words that they do not understand. Identify and relate to your audience. Meet the people afterward. Joke and be friendly, but be God's man.

Numerous times during the year, such as Christmas and Easter, during times of great personal need, such as death and divorce, the non-church public will automatically turn to the church. The place they go will be the man they know. Great opportunity for the ministry can be created if you are that man.

CHAPTER 39
Buy a Tent

Don't think that the people will not come to church just because the building, the location, the architecture are not the best. In the Marble Collegiate Church of New York City, in the First Baptist Church of Dallas, in the First Baptist church of Hammond, Indiana, and in the First Baptist church of Houston they come. These churches are old and they are not well located, but people like what they get, and they come.

Don't cross off the church. It is not the public that criticizes the church as much as it is the modern theologians. People still go to the structured church. Yet, it is often well in your evangelistic outreach to get out of the traditional four walls, into the residential sections where the people are. A tent revival, a stadium, coliseum, open-air or enclosed, but away from the ordinary, can be most attractive to the general public. A word of caution. Don't try to get by cheap. A chicken house with a few yellow lights *won't* get it. A cheap revival will cost, particularly outside of the church. One that is done well will pay for itself and do much good in evangelism as well as public relations.

Ben Loring, minister of evangelism at First Baptist, Houston, is charged with four major areas of evangelistic responsibility. I will outline two of them in this chapter and the next. They are high-school evangelism, mass evangelism, personal evangelism, and neighborhood evangelism. Neighborhood evangelism is done with a tent. No one particular area is the responsibility of the First Church of any city. It is under heaven charged with the responsibility of the entire city. Four months a year, June, July, August, and September, Mr. Loring will conduct sixteen weeks of tent revivals in sixteen different areas of the city. The plan:

1. Divide the city into sixteen major areas of population concentration.

2. Rent or borrow a vacant lot near major traffic arteries for use by the church for one week.

3. Commit all church families within that zone for six nights. It should be very clear to the people that although this is a four months effort, they will not be asked to go to a revival for four months. They are only being asked to attend the nights the tent is in their area.

4. Buy and errect a beautiful tent. Do not get a junky tent. Use a white tent with gold roping. Use Astroturf instead of sawdust. Have a nice public address system and decorate the parking lot with artificial flowers. Our tent is called the "First Baptist Chapel." The arrangements, flowers, lights, public address, music all should be professionally done. A half-shod presentation may do more harm than good.

5. Canvass the area two Saturdays in advance in shopping centers and private homes with leaflets, distributed by teen-age boys.

6. Commit all church families in the zone to a written

and telephone invitation to all zone people.

7. Friday night before the meeting, all church families meet with prospects, neighbors, and friends for a church-provided barbecue. The minister of evangelism, who will be preaching the meeting, will be in charge and speak. The church pastor, who will come in to every meeting and preach Friday night to close it out, will be at the concluding service of the previous weeks tent revival.

8. Zone families are committed to a 6:15 P.M. to 7:15 P.M. for nightly visitation during the meeting. Families can arrive with neighbors at the tent at 7:30 as there are no preservice prayer meetings, counselor sessions, or choir. Adequate and individual song leaders and pianists must be enlisted.

9. Pastor will close out the last night of each week. The concluding Friday's service to be followed by neighborhood fellowship and get-acquainted time with pastor in a local home of one of the members.

10. A church bus can be started the following Sunday morning at 9:00 to take converts and interested families to the downtown First Baptist Church. In some instances, missions could be begun instead.

This is a new inovation in outreach evangelism, and can obviously be more easily justified by a First Church than a suburban church. With some variation used, it could be profitably employed by almost any evangelistic group of people.

CHAPTER 40
Make Disciples

I have previously suggested an additional area of responsibility for the minister of evangelism or other qualified staff member or layman in the area of personal evangelism. He is charged with the responsibility of daily soul-winning visitation and training personal soul-winners. Pastor, you will never win your community by yourself. While you are to be ever at the job, the priority of training must be clearly established.

The imperative command to train men for a personal evangelism ministry comes from the apostle Paul. In giving the "job description" for Christian ministry in Ephesians 4:11–12, he says that all ministers, apostles, prophets, evangelists, pastors, and teachers have the *same* responsibilities and goal; that of "the perfecting of the saints for the work of the ministry" as the New English Bible puts it "to equip God's people for work in his service." The key words are "equip" and "ministry." We, as pastors, evangelists, and so forth have the command and privilege of equipping our people for the ministry God has for them— the winning of men to faith in Jesus Christ.

The sterling example of this principle is found in none other than our Lord Jesus Christ. With the responsibility of bringing God's message to the whole world, he selected twelve men and gave the majority of his earthly ministry to the thorough training and equipping of these men. From this apparently insignificant beginning has grown the Christian church. No greater priority should be given to any area of ministry than the training of our people to be personal soul-winners.

What is evangelism? Evangelism is that complete process by which the evangelized themselves become evangelists. In other words, merely winning men to Christ is not the end of our job. It is but the beginning. The process of evangelism includes making converts of sinners, disciples of converts, and soul-winners of disciples. It has been suggested that 20 percent of Christians never pray, 30 percent never go to church, 50 percent never give, 80 percent never attend prayer meeting, 90 percent never have family worship, and 99½ percent never win a soul to Christ! We speak in glowing terms of winning the world to Christ, and yet, we get farther and farther behind. Evangelist Billy Graham was asked, "If you were pastor of a large church in a principal city, what would be your plan of action?" He replied, "I would take eight or ten dedicated laymen and spend the majority of my time teaching them to win men to Christ and commit them in turn to teach others." This is the pattern that Jesus set and it should be our pattern as well.

There are nine basic principles involved in developing a program of training soul-winners.

1. *Select.*—Pick a handful of committed, willing, cooperative men. It may be as few as one or as many as twenty or thirty, but make it a very select group of men who have the desire to be soul-winners and a willingness to work.

Choose your own group of disciples. Follow the Master's example. Select them from all walks of life. The banker, lawyer, doctor, plumber, laborer. The main qualification is a burning desire to be used of God to win others.

2. *Commit.*—From the beginning, establish the priority of this program. Our churches are full of organizations that must be continually pumped up. We do not need another. The ones selected must be willing to commit themselves to personal evangelism as a *way of life*, not just a scheduled activity. Then, they must be committed to the job of training others in personal evangelism.

3. *Develop.*—Realize that it will take time to train even one man. It will not be done in a one week classroom training course. It may take a month, or two, or even longer to train a man to be a consistent, effective, soulwinner. Be ready to spend much time with your disciples.

4. *Equip.*—Teach them everything you know about soul winning. Expose them to every personal evangelism tool available. Use tracts, such as the "Four Spiritual Laws" from Campus Crusade for Christ, marked New Testaments, "How to Have a Full and Meaningful Life" and Scripture passages to memorize. Give them as much ammunition for spiritual battle as possible. Don't forget to not only teach them methods of evangelism, but also show them the heart, compassion, humility, prayerfulness, and dependency upon the Holy Spirit, which a soulwinner must have. Make this classroom time extremely valuable.

5. *Illustrate.*—Show them how to win people to Christ by taking them with you in your evangelistic visitation.

Spend the vast majority of your time in this area. As Dr. Kennedy of Coral Gables, Florida, says, "Evangelism cannot be taught, it must be caught." Expose them to every kind of witnessing situation possible: hospital, teen age, businessman, etc. Use the classroom time as a foundation for the "field experience." After your disciple has observed you in various witnessing experiences, give him the opportunity to take the initiative and you become the silent praying partner. After the visit, discuss the experience with him, giving suggestions where needed and much encouragement constantly. If you do not have enough lost to visit from your prospect file, then ask the disciple to make a list of his friends, neighbors, business associates that he would like to be saved, and go visit them together. Don't forget "cold turkey" evangelism either!

6. *Assign.*—After the initial training, give them a definite witnessing assignment. It may come from a list of lost people from your prospect file. It might be the evangelization of an area or neighborhood in your community. Perhaps you will assign a specific number of witnessing experiences to be engaged in within a week's time. However you choose to do it, give a definite assignment. People respond to concrete demands in Christian discipleship.

7. *Review.*—Maintain a check on the men that have been previously trained. If they are not constantly witnessing, find out what is wrong, correct it, and give them much encouragement. You can do this with tact without embarrassing the disciple. Simply invite him to go witnessing with you again. Spend time with him until he is

producing again. The principle of "assignment and re-view" is a long recognized truth in the world of successful business. In spiritual matters it is equally true. The spirit is often willing, but the flesh is weak. Usually we will only *do* what we are *expected* to do and what we are reminded to do. Keep your disciples on the ball. Review!

8. *Report.*—In connection with reviewing the men, the report session becomes invaluable. Set aside some time for a meeting of all men who are being trained, have been trained, and are training others. It may be weekly, bi-monthly, or monthly, but choose a time when *all* men involved can come. A 6:00 A.M. breakfast at a restaurant or hotel on a weekday may be necessary. In the meeting, let all the men report on their witnessing experiences since the last meeting. The purpose of the meeting is *encouragement* and *instruction.* If a man is letting down, the meeting will serve to fire him up again as he hears the experiences of others just like him. As men learn from their witnessing experiences, they can share with others in this meeting. No matter how few or how many are involved, have a *report meeting* consistently.

9. *Reproduce.*—The goal of your training is to equip men to win people to Christ and to teach them how to train other men. Make your methods simple enough that a person can use them in training another layman to become an effective soul-winner and trainer. The process is never completed—it is ongoing. For too long, we in the church have been working on the principle of addition (sometimes subtraction!). We must begin to operate on the principle of multiplication if we are to ever make an

impact on this world for Christ! The biblical imperative of multiplication is found in Paul's exhortation to young Timothy to commit the doctrine to faithful men who would be able to teach others.

Don't overlook the women of your church as you begin to train your people. Women who spend time at home provide an excellent opportunity for evangelism by the use of morning coffees or teas. Train a woman to be a soul-winner. Turn her loose in her community and watch what can happen! The command of our Lord was to make disciples of *all* of our flock. Whatever you do, make disciples!

CHAPTER 41

Use the Sunday School

Without question the Sunday School of your church can be the finest ongoing organization in Christendom for the enlistment, indoctrination, and winning of the lost. Two out of every three unsaved people enrolled in Sunday School will eventually be saved. But, only one out of every 230 people not enrolled in some Sunday School will ever be won to Christ.

For years, Arthur Flake's book *Building a Standard Sunday School* has been Bible in the field of religious education. His five steps still work.

1. Find the people.
2. Provide space.
3. Train leadership.
4. Enlarge the organization.
5. Divide and multiply.

At each of my last two pastorates our Sunday School attendance has quickly tripled by using these methods. While each situation may vary, the ultimate goal in Sunday School is teaching the most possible people in the best possible manner.

I think a word would be in order in defense of two of the most often misunderstood Sunday School procedures. The division of the classes and the segregating of the sexes. We have found through the years that people learn best in small groups where they are given personal attention and where there is time allowed for answering individual questions. People learn best by asking. Also, in a small class, a teacher can be in the home of every student every week. Learning of some particular situation or problem in the life or home of the student will enable the teacher to apply the lesson to meet particular needs and keep the Sunday School hour from becoming just another wasted hour in the week. Another principle is that it is often difficult to get a man to ask questions in front of his wife.

At this time, we are experimenting with a couples' class. By-and-large, I think it will be found, however, that a better overall quality of teaching can be done than in a smaller men's class or a smaller women's class. It should also be pointed to the skeptical prospective couple that the opening assembly is mixed as is Training Union, church, prayer meeting, and every other function of the church. It is only for an approximate thirty-five- or forty-minute teaching period during the entire church week that the couple is asked to separate. Again, however, let it be clearly stated that the organization is made for the people, not the people for the organization. If a persistent problem is found, making it impossible to enlist people to do a certain educational procedure, the structure should be changed to serve the needs of the people. Realizing the importance of fellowship, particularly in the lives of the teen-age student and the young married adult, it should also be understood that in a Sunday School class or department size unit, fellowship with our peers is best created.

A new couple may soon grow to feel much more a part of the total church family by personally knowing two or three other couples in a department than sitting with several hundred others in an auditorium. Sunday School breaks down the total organization into little pieces that you can get hold of. Here it is that through the weekly officers and teachers' meeting the work of the church can be promoted. In a financial pledge campaign, a Sunday School attendance goal, or any other overall objective by the church, it is possible to organize and mobilize the people through the existing structure of the Sunday School. Every department superintendent is a natural lieutenant for the commandeering of the troops. An "every member survey" is as simple in a one week period as the teacher's normal weekly visit to his class member.

In the past twelve months our budget was more than doubled and successfully pledged for the first time in history. The reason? The entire membership was broken down into existing Sunday School segments and contacted in person by teachers. During the same month, an all-time church record for foreign missions offering was established. It is a must for the preacher to meet weekly with his superintendents. Here, plans can be made, inspiration given, problems solved, directions established through the entire organization of the church. The Sunday School can also be a most effective tool in feeding evangelistic prospects into the church services. In using the Sunday School for evangelism, stewardship, discipleship, and leadership training, remember this! *Enrolment is the most important statistic you have in your church.* Conversions, baptisms, and growth all stem from enrolment.

My first day in Houston the church attempted to welcome me with a Sunday School attendance of 1,400, the highest in years. This would have been an increase from over 800 the previous Sunday. The grand day came and the great attendance was announced—781. Monday morning I went to the Sunday School records and found out why 1,400 in Sunday School was impossible. We barely had 1,400 enrolled. The larger the church, the smaller the percentage, but the average healthy growing Sunday School can expect to peak at around 55 percent of its enrolment. The obvious answer to our dilemma and to that of every church earnestly desiring to increase its Sunday School attendance is simply to increase Sunday School enrolment. We did two things that immediately increased our Sunday School attendance.

1. In the Sunday School classes, in the morning service, over the telephone, on the sidewalks, anywhere and everywhere we enrolled everyone who was willing to join our Sunday School. I hope that you do not make people come to your Sunday School three times before you enrol them. In case you haven't heard, that idea went out with high buttoned shoes! I will enrol anyone under any condition, anytime, anywhere, whether he be Jew, Catholic, or whatever in my Sunday School. He then becomes someone's personal responsibility, and a serious-minded teacher is immediately charged with the responsibility of

his personal involvement.

2. We discovered that 900 church members were not enrolled in Sunday School. We sent them a letter telling them the importance of Sunday School membership as well as church membership. Each letter returned contained a returned card not saying "do you want to join our Sunday School?" But, "please fill out if you do not want to." Forty-five people returned the cards and 855 new persons were added to the existing Sunday School rolls. In addition to this, everyone who joins the church is automatically enrolled in Sunday School. An inside survey, when all Sunday morning church attenders on a given Sunday are asked to submit names of prospects, can also increase enrolment. Prospects are given to a church visitor and are visited and enrolled in the homes. It is to be made very clear that the prospect is not joining the church, merely the Sunday School—that great happy hunting ground for an aggressive prospect Sunday School teacher. In six months this plan increased our Sunday School enrolment over 1,000 and weekly average attendance by over 500.

Sunday School is the place to enrol prospects, to teach and train in the word of God, and to get them primed and prepared for a warm morning service where decisions can be made. Sunday School is where the offerings are received, it is where discipleship is taught, maturity is gained, stewardship is taught, maturity reached, fellowship promoted, and goals reached. Tomorrow's tithers, soul-winners, teachers, deacons, and preachers are today's Sunday School members.

CHAPTER 42
Buy a Softball

A church recreation program has a five-fold usefulness.

1. The initial attraction of prospects.
2. Cultivation of lasting Christian friendships.
3. Teaching of Christian principles in life.
4. Wholesome recreational outlet.
5. Just plain fun!

Every church contains varying degrees of spirituality in its membership. You can teach and preach for fifty years, but there are some people that will never mature sufficiently to win souls, sing in a choir, or teach a class. But, these people can be enlisted. There is something that everyone can do. Someone in your church will paint that sign, fix that nail, cook that meal, or coach that team. And, coaching a team that attracts and enlists prospects can be a good witness.

I have probably baptized thirty to fifty men over the past six years strictly from our recreational programs. Begin early in enlisting managers, coaches, enrolling in leagues, and purchasing new equipment. Build teams such as softball, basketball, and volleyball for women as well as men. Start young children's recreational leagues. Encourage church members to enlist non-Christians to play on the team. Begin each game with prayer and finish each game with refreshments and a brief time of fellowship. Encourage all of the players to become well acquainted with the non-church players. Some kind of rule should be established requiring the nonmember player to attend a certain amount of church services.

Purchase uniforms. A good team identity with the name of the church proudly displayed on the uniforms not only builds pride in your people, but it can give the prospect a sense of the joy of fellowship that could be his in belonging. The manager and players should visit for fellowship and witness in the home of a non-church player weekly. A word of caution: Do not forget the man after the season is over. If he is not won to Christ or does not join the church, it is not very likely that he ever will if you fail to see him between seasons.

Families of players should be encouraged to attend the games and sit together. The church members' wives and children can go by and pick up the family of the non-church member, arriving in time for the game. Here is another possibility of prospect cultivation. Incidentally, the best time to commit them to be ready for you to pick them up for Sunday School the following Sunday is that night when you drop them off at their home.

Give adequate recognition, announcement, and rewards to team members in the Sunday morning services and include the prospects' names in all recognition. Have the team sit together as special guests of the pastor at the beginning of the season. Have an all-church fellowship with team recognition at the end of the season. Remind the team consistently that Christian fellowship and not merely winning is the primary reason for the existence of the church team. Arguing and complaining, let alone profanity or fighting is never to be tolerated on the church athletic field. Every player should be concerned primarily not just with victory, but safety, Christian fellowship, and a genuine God-honoring experience.

Recreational involvement for senior adults should also be explored. Many churches have begun a fun and fellowship time mornings for older people. The possibilities are endless and the results most gratifying.

An additional note of suggestion. Number and store all athletic materials in a safe and proper place at the end of the season. Clean and mothproof all uniforms. A fee should be charged each individual who plays on a church league team. They are much more likely to respect the equipment and be consistently in attendance if they are paying for the privilege.

As pastor, attend the games yourself and/or play. It is a terrific opportunity for fellowship with your men. As center fielder on our church softball team when I left Del City to move to Houston, the team presented me a gold cup commemorating my catching the most line drives in the history of the league, *with my forehead and shins.* You do not have to be the best to play, but you can do one of the best things to play with the prospects and men of your church on a church ball team. You will win the hearts of your people and it may help you to win the souls of men.

CHAPTER 43

Buy a Camera

Someone in your church is a camera bug and well qualified in taking pictures. While one picture may or may not be worth a thousand words, it is certainly worth a lot to that prospect or member who sees his picture, his family's picture, or something in which he is very interested in the church paper or somewhere in the Sunday School or church building.

A good church paper should be loaded with pictures. Pictures of new members, pictures of sporting events, revivals, coming speakers, teachers or deacons being honored, etc. A hot prospect's name may even be added to the church mailing list and receive the church paper weekly. Church papers should be distributed on visitation nights to prospective families. A library of one to two hundred pictures collected through the years of exciting church groups and activities could be sprinkled two or three a week throughout the church paper and made available to the prospective members.

Get a good grade of camera, use proper lighting, take your time, and get good pictures. Fuzzy, dark prints in a church paper may suggest that everything the church does is sloppy and careless and could possibly do more harm than good.

Through the years we have used the power of the camera most effectively and have found some important truths about a picture ministry.

1. Use good equipment.

2. Use a qualified man.

3. Invest in some developing equipment. It can save lots of money.

4. Use proper lighting.

5. Except for Sunday morning new members, catch people being themselves. Do not use a pose.

6. Never take crowd shots from the back.

7. Never take crowd shots seated. Standing crowds taken from the front will fill up the empty seats and make the picture look better.

8. Take very little time to interrupt a service just for pictures.

9. Publish the pictures when they are taken. People want to see what you took.

10. Place clear and adequate captions explaining who, what, where, when, how many, and why when the pictures are published.

11. Keep a good library of previous pictures. They can be a most invaluable asset in future publications and promotional pieces.

12. Label adequately. Do not trust yourself to remember ten years later who was in that picture or when it was taken. It is also important in newspaper advertising not to clutter up the ad with too many words. Remember that white space sells and so do pictures.

A camera will help add a fresh and modern dimension to the public relations program of your church.

CHAPTER 44
Use That Evangelist

The United States Government Bureau of Statistics registers over 1,200 religions, sects, denominations, and cults in the United States. Nearly everyone of them has their equivalent of a full-time evangelist. Every denomination has the full-time Christian worker who is talented, dedicated, and capable, but not always busily employed. In my own Southern Baptist denomination there are probably well in excess of 300 full-time vocational evangelists. Many of these men are new to the field of evangelism and have extra time during the early years of their ministry. Nearly every evangelist has some time off around May, June, December, January, and February, the slower months for revival meetings. With varying degrees of actual church relationships, the talents and services of the full-time evangelist can be used in the program of the local church.

In Del City, Oklahoma, we had seven full-time Southern Baptist evangelists and three full-time evangelistic singers. It was our pleasure to recommend, support, and pray for these men, listen to the reports of their meetings when they were home, and minister to their families in their absense. We furnished all ten of them with free stationery, a free office, and hopefully some status in the secular world by being a staff evangelist in an established church rather than being an independent evangelist. And oh, how God blessed us for that! It would be impossible to measure the blessings that came to us for doing it. It was our plan to eventually pay for the health insurance and retirement program of these men as well. From time to time during their off-weeks, they were hired by our church to assist in revival visitation, hospital visitation, prospect visitation, and for baptism follow-up visitation. Fifteen dollars per day or one hundred dollars per week may not be a lot of money, but it can be a great blessing to an evangelist who may be off a few weeks without a meeting at Christmas time and he will certainly be a blessing to you and your church. Through the years we have tried to help the evangelist. We have used them and it has been mutually beneficial to them and to us. God has blessed us for being a blessing to his good men, the evangelists. "Go thou and do likewise."

CHAPTER 45

Use the Telephone

There has got to be an easier way, and there usually is if you will put your mind to it. One of the best, easy ways is to do it over the telephone. Ideas to the staff, the secretaries, and the office can be quickly conveyed in this manner. Every time you have a new thought and idea, something that should be done immediately, someone to be seen, a name to be recorded, pick up that telephone. Problems can be headed off by the telephone. An appointment cancelled or changed by use of the telephone can save endless hours in a difficult problem of scheduling.

Schedule out-of-office appointments by areas. Do not run back and forth across town. Most people, when informed well in advance by a courteous telephone call, will be most happy to change the time of an appointment to more easily fit your schedule. A telephone call can be much more personal than a dictated letter and it certainly is much more convenient, much quicker, and much less expensive. In a matter of fifteen minutes you can:

1. Call a sick member in the hospital.

2. Encourage a discouraged Sunday School teacher.

3. Congratulate a high school or college student on an award.

4. Remind a superintendent of the urgency of next Sunday morning's attendance.

While it is well to visit every sick person in the hospital at least once a week or two or three times if possible, in less serious cases the patient will usually always be more than understanding if a courteous telephone call is made telling them of your interest and concern. Pray over the telephone. A distraught mother or a depressed sick person can find immediate help from a sincere telephone call from the pastor. Happy birthday calls to Sunday School workers and deacons can be most helpful.

For years I have called prospects on Saturday night between 7:00 and 10:00. Call that prospect. Tell him how happy you are that he came to church last Sunday and how you attempted to visit him this week but was unable to do so. Ask about his family. Tell him about the church. Urge him to come again. If he shows serious interest, but does not join the next day, a Sunday afternoon visit in person may insure a new member for Sunday night. It is important that the prospect not feel that he is that, merely a prospect, just another statistic for your church. Let him know that you are genuinely interested in every area of his life. Ask about his job, children, hobbies, and interests. If the prospect is ill, visit him. If there is a new baby or new promotion, or award, call with congratulations. It is a gesture that will not soon be forgotten.

Setting up important meetings and keeping distant appointments can be greatly enhanced by the use of long distance phone calls. People are busy. They forget to answer their mail or they are delayed. A ten day delay in answering a letter may make it necessary for you to hold up on a hundred other related details. A dollar spent now may save ten hours time later.

By the way, preacher, call your wife. Call her two or three times during the day. Tell her where you are, tell her you will be late, and by all means keep in touch with the office. They need to know where you are at all times. Personal contacts, letters, visits, the telephone call, can all be of great assistance to the modern-day pastor. A call to a pastor friend can bring a good illustration for Sunday's sermon as easily as a call to an aged mother on her birthday can bring a blessing to you both. It is good business to keep in touch.

not suggest sacrificing quality for the sake of quantity. And I certainly do not endorse quality at the sacrifice of quantity. The two can go hand in hand, but the devil is defeating you if he has you using the excuse that you are only interested in quality and are ignoring evangelistic outreach.

3. The priority of evangelism over social action must be clearly established. Did not our Lord himself in the ultimate authoritative statement on the matter say, "What is a man profited if he gain the whole world and lose his own soul?" Who is better off today, Lazarus, the rich man in hell, or Dives, the poor man in heaven? Which was more important, their fifty years on earth or their endless state in eternity? Jesus left nothing in doubt about that. There is no question about it. While we do want to minister to the whole man, the soul is more important than the body. It is the devil's lie to get us to believe anything else. One second in eternity will clearly validate that fact. And yet, the two are not necessarily clearly separated. I take great exception with the man who says the evangelicals care nothing for the material matters of man. When a man is saved, ideally many things happen. He may restore stolen property, thus help balance the economy. He will certainly work harder and be more honest at his job when helping to earn his salary and helping to stabilize inflation. He will keep a neater yard, empty trash properly, refrain from dumping crude oil into the lakes, and burning down the forests. A Christian is good for ecology. He will need less psychiatrists, less sleeping pills, and less ulcer medicine. He will love his

neighbor regardless of race, color, or creed. Why? Because the preacher preached on ecology and race religion? Because he marched in a parade? No. Not at all. Because he is saved. He is a new creation. A new creature in Jesus Christ. Only a fool would say that winning men to Christ is not a priority and does not possess a total and absolute involvement in the solution to social matters.

Let's keep the record straight. In the hearts of men and in the plan of God, in the world, in the church, and in the preachers' life, evangelism is priority.